ETERNAL BLACK EYE

Toshua L. Cornwell-Clark M.S.

Sociologist, Social Scientist

DEDICATION

This book is dedicated to my maternal grandmother, Ma'dear, and my ancestors, the people who came before me, who suffered while paving the way so that I could thrive. Your relentless resilience gives me ambition, your perseverance and determination gave me a road map. None of your labor was in vain. I am thankful to you, and your legacy lives on through me!

CONTENTS

ACKNOWLEDGEMENTS

I want to thank the Black woman who influenced me the most, and that woman is my mom, Lynn, whom I call "Yen". She poured love into me and allowed me to become the woman that I am today. My mom taught me to stand on my own and to not follow the crowd, but instead, move the crowd, and if there is no path, then carve one out for myself. My mother is brilliant, a divine gift from God, she pours knowledge, wrapped with love, into everyone. I could never thank her enough for all that she does!

I also want to thank my dad, Joshua, for understanding me, always being consistent in my life, and giving me an example of what a man should be.

I must thank my husband, Gentleman Jimmy, for being the balance and the harmony to this song called my life; his patience brings me peace and harmony.

I am also very blessed to have my brilliant Sister Keisha who always shows up in sincerity. To my incredibly smart nieces Nicole (my big baby) & Mariah (my sweetheart), my nephews Ronnie (w/ the top hat), and my super savvy Derick (Tikki) who keep me on my toes, I love you all.

I am honored to have my friends, Angela Nixon (one of the most intellectual women I know) who really gets my essence. D.D. who is so reliable. To my "good-good gurl-friend"; Dr. Keisha Clark, my travel buddy, who encourages me, propels me out of my comfort zone, and is truly a gem who does not extract, but rather deposits into my life. I am so happy that you are all my tribe.

I would be remiss if I did not acknowledge all the hair stylists who maintain and enhance the beauty of our people. Particularly, Latanya Williams, and her daughter Candace Williams (owners of Premier One on One Salon), Janet Miller (owner of Glorious Strands Salon), Martel Moon (owner of Highly Favored Salon), and Latera Pugh (an extraordinary Cosmetology Educator) who I can always count on, all of whom have contributed their expertise to the beauty industry. Thank you!

FOREWORD

I feel like I'm having an early morning musing or late-night nosh on this juicy bitter subject matter with my dear friend and co-laborer, to the witnessing of a people's dis-ease. From the time we met, there was a common communing of spirits between the two of us. Not only did we share heritage as we can gather from the external; there was also something else present, a burst of joy, light, and shouting of our souls that we had found the one who understood the burden of carrying the demanding torch of being a truth-teller of our stories.

My colonial credentials are Dr. Keisha Clark. Leading an Office of Equity in San Diego County, I am an anti-racist activist in the government sector, and a freedom fighter in my private life. I know full well why my friend asked me to write this foreword because the idea was birthed from our many conversations about race and racism. We both deeply understand the consequences of this work and she was determined to capture and cement the downloaded messages she receives from her source.

As you hang on to every page, you will discover that Toshua as an author is as passionate as she is sharp. She holds no bars and clearly illustrates her message so that you, the reader will feel it in the pit of your stomach and the frog in your throat. She most certainly may offend you purposely as she does not dilute or sanitize this serving to fit your palate; it is hard to swallow for a reason. She may mix you a cocktail to wash it down, but the aftertaste is nothing but nasty and vile.

There are two types of readers who will be impacted by the words on these pages, the intended victim and the unintended victim. Make no mistake, none of us get away unscathed. To the intended victim, use Toshua's words to enlighten you of your current condition and rebirth yourself in ancestral community. To the unintended victims, own your birthright and take your medicine. In a world of "comfort", I am so glad that I've met Toshua who doesn't mind getting dirty and, in the nooks, and crannies of life, peeking around the corner in the dark alleys to shine the bright light of truth.

This book highlights the lows of life for the African Diaspora. The history, present, and future are interwoven to form a tapestry of narrative for the Global Majority's experience especially in the America's. Due to the stratification of hue-mans, ancestral and communal healing has not and will not occur. The utter confusion about American values versus African values have wreaked havoc physically, emotionally, mentally, psychologically, financially, etc. There is no system in America that racism has not touched.

Toshua uses storytelling, an African tradition, to illustrate moment by moment racist instances of the perpetual re-wounding of the black eye. When you place this in context and perspective, Black individuals should be in awe of our resilience. Personal and professional examples as well as observations inform this Based on a True Story experience. Born out of the loins of her soul, Toshua could no longer hold onto this information without bringing it forth as a gift to her readers.

Beyond Toshua's personal interest in the subject matter, she was born into a Black body. Toshua has studied in the halls of colonialism as well as worked for many organizations that perpetuated the injuries she is sharing through these pages. She has studied to show herself approved because even when the adversary is trying to hide the truth or feed you misinformation, she was determined to excavate her-story. She shares these stories on many platforms from speaking, to presentations, workshops, and books.

In closing, I would not endorse this book if I didn't wholeheartedly recommend and trust the source.

-Dr. Keisha Clark

ABSTRACT

This manuscript isn't just a recounting of injustices, it's a powerful unmasking of history's most persistent systemic inequalities. From the chains of chattel slavery to the silent weight of internalized racism, it exposes how centuries-old systems of oppression have shaped the modern Black experience. But beyond exposing these injustices, it asks the most urgent question: How do we heal?

With razor-sharp insight, this book peels back the layers of systemic racism, unravelling the roots of colorism, Eurocentric beauty ideals, and the fractures in Black solidarity. It journeys through the echoes of intergenerational trauma passed down through generations, unpacking its grip on self-identity, community bonds, and societal structures. Inspired by personal lived experiences and the groundbreaking research that I have done as a sociologist focused on anti-Black racism. The narrative confronts these legacies with fearless clarity.

But this isn't just history, it's a rallying cry for transformation. Infused with vivid storytelling, cultural reflections, and poignant moments of truth, the manuscript celebrates resilience and reclamation. From the hidden language of "B-talk" to the collective power of cultural renaissance, it offers not just an understanding of the past but a roadmap for breaking free from it.

This is a story about injustice, yes—but more importantly, it's a story about liberation. It's a blueprint for reclaiming identity, rewriting the narrative, and embracing the beauty, strength, and unity that's always existed within. The wounds of history demand acknowledgement and this manuscript dares you to face them and then do the work to heal.

Keywords: Injustices, Systemic inequalities, Chattel slavery, Internalized racism, Oppression, Systemic racism, Colorism, Eurocentric beauty ideals, Intergenerational trauma, Resilience.

INTRODUCTION

THE WOUND THAT NEVER HEALED

In embarking on this journey, my foremost intent is to educate, heal, and strengthen the global majority of the African diaspora; i.e. Black Folks. From the onset, let us dispel the fabricated term "Black-on-Black crime." Consider this: you will never hear references to "white-on-white crime," "Asian-on-Asian crime," or "Mexican-on-Mexican crime." Why? Because crime happens in proximity. While this book does not focus on crime in the traditional sense, it examines a more profound crime: a crime against humanity. It explores the enduring trauma that Americans of African descent and the global majority of the African diaspora, i.e. Black folks, have been forced to endure.

This book opens the door to a conversation often avoided: the impact of internalized racism. Pervasive yet seldomly discussed, internalized racism affects nearly every Black person. Its roots lie in the scars left by chattel slavery, colonialism, neocolonialism, social stratification, institutional racism, and structural racism. For instance, studies have shown that Black individuals often internalize negative stereotypes perpetuated by media or societal norms, leading to decreased self-esteem or even discriminatory behaviors within their communities.

Together, we will unpack this trauma, layer by layer, beginning with clear definitions of two key concepts: prejudice and racism.

PREJUDICE VS. RACISM

According to Merriam-Webster, prejudice is a negative attitude or feeling toward a person or group formed before any direct experience with them. I like to correlate the word prejudice to the two words "pre-judge" (a strong dislike). *For example*, someone might assume that older individuals lack the technological skills of younger generations or believe that certain physical attributes equate to personality traits. These biases, while natural, can have harmful consequences when left unchecked.

Racism, however, goes deeper. Merriam-Webster defines racism as the belief that race fundamentally determines human traits and capacities and that racial differences create inherent superiority. Additionally, racism is characterized by the systemic oppression of one racial group for the social, economic, and political benefit of another. Racism essentially equates to the 3-P's, prejudice plus power, with the key word being power.

Take housing discrimination, For example. A 2022 report revealed that Black families are still 2.5 times more likely than white families to be denied mortgages, even when financial qualifications are comparable. This disparity isn't just a coincidence; it's a result of structural racism and prejudice backed by the power to enforce inequality. The benefits from homeownership have not been shared equally. In the second quarter of 2022, the homeownership rate for white households was 75 percent compared to 45 percent for Black households (2022).

This is where the "3 P's" come into play: prejudice plus power. It's not just about disliking another group, it's about having the power to control their opportunities, livelihoods, and access to resources. Whether through redlining, voter suppression, or disparities in education, this combination of prejudice and power has created systemic barriers that continue to affect marginalized communities.

Now, let's return to the question: Can Black people be prejudiced? The answer is yes. However, by Merriam-Webster's definition, Black people cannot be racist. Racism requires the power to enforce prejudice on a systemic level. Without that power dynamic, any racism becomes internalized; a painful reflection of the historical and structural forces that perpetuate inequality.

For instance, consider the phenomenon of "colorism" within Black communities. This preference for lighter skin tones, rooted in colonial history and reinforced by media representation, is a form of internalized racism. It highlights how systemic oppression can infiltrate personal and communal attitudes, further dividing those it was designed to subjugate.

INTERNALIZED RACISM: A LEGACY OF CHATTEL SLAVERY

Internalized racism and colorism are not just individual struggles; they are deeply rooted issues that have quietly endured across generations, profoundly shaping self-perception, relationships, and unity within the African diaspora. These issues can be traced back to deliberate psychological strategies employed during colonialism, strategies designed to devalue the African aesthetic and injure the collective psyche, especially regarding Black features and identity.

According to Social Scientist, professor, and author, Dr. Joy Degruy, "history affects behaviors, and are largely related to trans-generational adaptations associated with traumas, past and present from ongoing oppression" (Degruy, 2005). A theory and framework that Dr. Degruy has employed, termed "Post Traumatic Slave Syndrome" PTSS, which would later become the subject of her groundbreaking book, Post-Traumatic Slave Syndrome: America's Legacy of Enduring Injury and Healing, serves as a lens to examine how these historical wounds manifest in modern times. By shedding light on these often-unspoken experiences, we can begin to understand their origins and work collectively toward healing.

Imagine colonialism, structural racism, and institutional oppression as repeated blows to the eye, compounded by the relentless force of police brutality. Such unyielding violence leaves an "Eternal Black Eye," symbolizing the collective trauma endured by Black communities over centuries. This metaphor reflects the pain and the challenges of healing, but it also signals the resilience required to confront and dismantle these forces.

To address internalized racism, we must first educate ourselves about its roots. Unpacking this issue is like peeling a metaphorical onion; each layer reveals the systemic and purposeful strategies that fractured unity within the Black community. These strategies were not accidents, they were deliberate acts of control designed to maintain colonial dominance.

Education is our first step in addressing these issues. To face and tear down the remaining powerful impacts of internalized racism, one would have to go back into history and look for its representations. Unpacking this is like peeling the layers of a metaphorical onion; with each layer, it reveals itself to be systemic and purposeful strategies made to fracture unity within the Black community.

This book will discuss a theoretical concept and or a sociological framework that I created; and termed as "The Colonial Costume". The colonial costume is metaphoric for a position that one takes upon himself as an upholder of colonialism, meaning that they have taken on the persona, that of the colonizer. That person is sociologically framed as "the actor".

The actor has psychologically disassociated themselves from the African diaspora, seemingly seeking complete detachment.

The actor provides no psychological safety for the Black collective … especially those who culturally present as, "Too Black". The actor has developed imposter syndrome, playing a mental game of tug-of-war with themselves, as to who they are and who they wish to be. They wear the colonial costume neatly tucked in, so as not to make themselves readily identifiable. However, their interactions are indicative of neocolonial cosplay, and instantaneously their mask is removed and ah-ha, the actor and his colonial costume become recognizable.

For example, contemporary practices such as skin bleaching or adherence to Eurocentric beauty standards highlight the lingering effects of these colonial strategies. As Seaton (2022) notes, internalized racism is "invisible yet omnipresent," its insidious nature making it challenging to identify and confront. These behaviors are not merely cosmetic; they reflect a deeper psychological battle, a tug-of-war between cultural identity and the desire to conform to imposed ideals.

Uncovering how these divisive tactics were designed and implemented, we can recognize their lingering effects on our thoughts and behaviors today.

WHAT IS INTERNALIZED RACISM?

To fully grasp internalized racism, we must first define it. It is the intrapersonal form of racism an internalization or endorsement of negative stereotypes about one's ethnoracial group and oneself based on one's identity. According to James and Iyer (2024), internalized racism manifests in various ways, including embracing White beauty standards, rejecting ancestral culture, and accepting the limitations placed on one's ethnic-racial group.

Seaton further elaborates, stating that internalized racism often leads to self-devaluation and a loss of connection to one's cultural heritage. "Internalized racism is not so easy to see, to count, to measure and does not involve one perpetrator and one corresponding victim but instead has been adopted and resides in the psyche of targets" (Seaton et al., 2022).

This profound observation underscores the psychological depth of this issue, making it a complex and pervasive force that requires both introspection and collective effort to overcome.

This book invites readers to embark on a journey a metaphorical unpeeling of the onion and unpacking of the suitcase of internalized racism. Together, we will trace the origins of these divisive tactics, examining how they were designed and implemented during colonial times. By understanding these strategies, we can recognize their lingering effects on our thoughts and behaviors today. Education and collective action are our first steps toward dismantling these enduring systems of oppression and reclaiming unity within the Black community.

Through this lens, we can confront the weight of the "Colonial Costume" and its pervasive influence, empowering individuals to shed this burden and embrace the richness of their heritage. The process is challenging, but it is essential for fostering resilience, unity, and healing.

MY FAMILY LANGUAGE: "B-TALK"

As a little girl growing up in San Diego, I always admired the variety of skin tones I saw amongst my mom and my aunties, who I call Auinnies (pronounced a-knees). Their complexions range from high yella (light-skinned), caramel/golden brown skin, to the deepest cocoa skin like a beautiful plum. They were all beautiful.

Now my Auinnie Delphine, who was high yella, with the most gorgeous hazel eyes, with soft hair, wore #3 burgundy lipstick and always smelled good like she had freshly bathed in plumeria and lightly scented with Lutice perfume or Imari perfume from Avon.

I was very close to her; I would lay across her bed, and we would talk for hours. She always told me her father was a "Geechee/Creole man". At the time, I thought this meant he was a mix of French and Black heritage. It wasn't until much later that I learned the term "Geechee" refers to the Gullah Geechee people, who developed their language during the 18th century.

Ironically, my family speaks an unknown language, called "B-talk". My grandmother Ma'dear would be rolling over in her grave if she knew I was telling you this, especially in a book. But it is true, Ma'dear and my aunts always spoke "B-talk" to us. Some words came out so fast that sometimes, we children could barely make out exactly what they were saying. We often spoke B-talk in public when we didn't want someone to be privy to our conversation. Not that we were necessarily saying something terrible, it was just a way to keep the conversation between us.

Languages like "B-talk" are, in many ways, about resilience, which is a way of maintaining autonomy and connection in the face of systemic oppression. These hidden languages, often born of necessity, became cultural treasures passed down through generations.

In 2023, my husband Jimmy and I were on vacation with my sister Keisha and her husband, we had an unforgettable experience. While at Sangster Airport in Montego Bay, Jamaica, I needed to tell Keisha something urgently from across the room. Instinctively, I yelled in B-talk, and she responded in kind. The entire airport seemed to freeze, heads turning as people tried to decode what they'd just heard. Our husbands, perplexed, asked, "What was that?" Keisha and I realized they'd never heard us speak B-talk before. That moment was both amusing and profound, as it highlighted how much this unique language was woven into our identities.

As an adult, I had become interested in the origins of "B-talk", our family language. I'd recently seen a video on social media where a Black woman mentioned that her family speaks a secret language that her enslaved ancestors spoke to communicate without the slave masters knowing what was being said.

I couldn't help but wonder, could my family language have originated in the same manner. So, I called my oldest

living aunt "Aunt Bennie-Mae," down in Houston, Texas, who is in her 80's and has her right mind. I asked her, "Aunt Bennie, where did b-talk come from?" She replied, "Oh, I don't know, but I do know that my Uncle Jean used to say, I ain't speaking that slave language."

I froze as if I had just uncovered a missing puzzle piece to a lost treasure. This was our family treasure. Sadly, our language has become a dying art, as our relatives no longer or, if so, rarely speak B-talk to the children in our family. However, I am very intentional, and we speak it to my 8-year-old great nephew Derick (who I call Tikki), who also understands and speaks it.

The rediscovery of "B-talk" and its many variants of family languages is a real reminder of just how strong and creative our enslaved ancestors were. A need to communicate out of the reach of enslavers, these survival strategies are no different in many ways from what continues to shape Black life today.

Now, back to my Aunt Delphine. I would lie across her bed as she and my mom Lynn (Yen) would tell me stories of their childhood. My mother's childhood experiences are imprinted so vividly on her memory, that when she and Auinnie Delphine reminisced, I could picture it as though I were there. One story that always stood out to me was about their grandmother, my maternal great-grandmother Angie-Mae, born in 1895.

GREAT-GRANDMA ANGIE-MAE

This story of Great-Grandmother Angie-Mae reflects the long-lasting psychological wounds that are a result of systemic oppression. She preferred her lighter-skinned grandchildren because of internalized racism imposed by colonialism and colorism. It is a sad legacy that haunts many families to this day, perpetuating divisions that prevent healing.

Angie-Mae was a fair-skinned woman (high yella). My mom recalls being a little girl and peeping around the corner and catching a rare glimpse of Grandma Angie Mae brushing her long, wavy grey hair; as my mom tip-toed and stood from afar admiring her beautiful hair, she made sure to not make a sound because if Grandma Angie Mae realized that she was watching, she would surely holler, "OUT, you go back outside and play with the other kids!" My mom decided that she had better get out of there and return to playing outside with the other kids because she did not want to get into any trouble.

When my grandmother Ma'dear went to work, she would leave her kids (my mom & aunts) to be cared for by her mom, great grandma Angie-Mae. The darker-skinned grandchildren were made to stay outside in the blazing hot Texas sun all day. Meanwhile, the lighter-skinned kids were allowed inside for a cold drink and lunch. This blatant colorism was painful, but back then, children didn't dare talk back nor question adults or complain. They simply dealt with it.

One day, Aunt Delphine, got fed up with Grandma Angie-Mae's shit, she grabbed both of grandma's arms and shock her and demanded, "Stop treating us so mean!" Though Aunt Delphine was light-skinned herself, she stood up for her darker-skinned siblings and cousins. Her act of defiance earned her a severe punishment, or in her words "I got a good old ass whoopin" but she also told me, "It was well worth it."

Amidst such divisions, the acts of resistance and courage, one instance being Aunt Delphine standing up to Grandma Angie-Mae, serve as a reminder of that unwavering spirit within the community. Such acts of defiance, though minute, are representative of an ongoing struggle to confront and dismantle internalized biases.

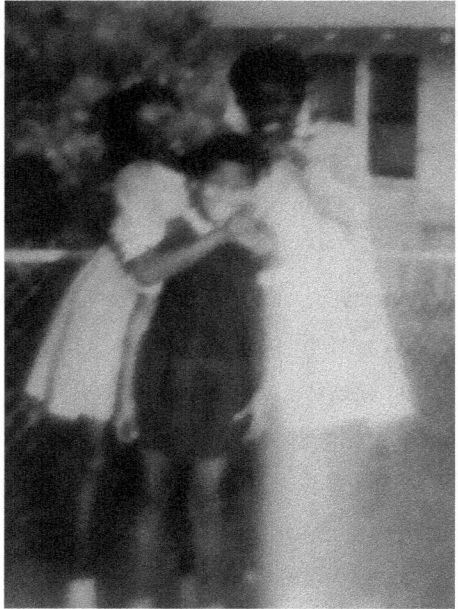

Sadly, many people who had seen the atrociousness of colonialism had internalized the very biases that were meant to destroy us as a people. I feel sad that my great-grandmother couldn't escape colorism. However, I value her as a woman being able to endure all that she had to experience at the wicked hands of systemic oppression.

Great-grandmother Angie-Mae's story highlights the pervasive impact of colorism, a legacy of pain. Healing from this history requires acknowledging the damage caused and committing to dismantling harmful ideologies.

On a Sunday morning, Great-grandmother Angie-Mae went to church, and kneeled at the pew, to pray before taking her seat, as this is not uncommon, pastors do this all the time.

According to the elders of my family, the church service was jumping, the spirit was high, the choir was singing to the highest of worship, and no one noticed that great-grandmother had not gotten up off her knees to take her seat. She had died, yes, she died right there in the church on her knees in prayer; this was on Sunday, July 23rd, 1972. For her, the colorism died that day, but sadly, for others, it lived on.

Healing isn't just about education; it's about creating psychological safety and addressing the trauma caused by systemic and interpersonal racism. Through personal narratives and actionable steps, this book aims to inspire collective healing and transformation.

Understanding our history is crucial for addressing the challenges we face today. By examining the past, we can uncover valuable lessons that guide us toward unity and empathy. A strong community is built on respect and appreciation for our diverse skin tones, hair textures, and cultural experiences. Together, we can challenge oppressive structures and create a brighter future.

The structure of this book is designed to guide readers through this journey of understanding and healing:

Education alone is not enough. Healing is a vital part of this process. Acknowledging the psychological damage caused by institutional racism and the interpersonal trauma that fuels internalized racism and colorism is something that we, as a community, must address directly. Through personal narratives, reflections, and actionable steps, this book aims to enlighten these deep-seated issues and collectively find a healing space through psychological safety. Healing is a personal and collective journey; together, we can support one another in this transformative process, leading to a brighter future.

Ultimately, the goal is to strengthen our community. When we understand and heal from the wounds inflicted by the legacy of slavery, we empower ourselves and those around us.

A strong community is built on unity, respect, and appreciation for our rich diversity of skin tones, hair textures, and cultural experiences. By fostering a sense of solidarity, we can more effectively challenge external oppressive structures and create a brighter future for future generations. Understanding our history is crucial for addressing the challenges we face today.

The barriers we encounter stem from long-standing systemic issues and divisions, highlighting the importance of unity and empathy as we progress. Examining the past reveals valuable lessons that guide us toward a brighter future. This historical insight empowers us to challenge and dismantle harmful ideologies like internalized racism and colorism allowing us to build a more inclusive and understanding society. Together, we can create meaningful change and foster a more equitable world!

The structure of this book is carefully designed to guide the reader through this journey of understanding and healing:

1. **Understanding the Root Causes:** Explore the historical foundations of colorism and how colonialism planted seeds of division.

2. **The Impact of Internalized Racism:** Examine how systemic oppression manifests in interpersonal relationships and self-perception.

3. **Manifestations of Texturism:** Here, we examine how these ingrained beliefs manifest in our daily lives, from the language we use to our perceptions of beauty and worth. Society pathologizes tightly coiled hair, leaving us to feel as though it is something less desirable and that we need to alter our natural hair texture and curl pattern by straightening it, thus forcing us to conform to the Euro-standard of beauty. By identifying these patterns, we become more aware of their presence and impact. Don't get me wrong, as a licensed cosmetologist since 1994 and a professor of cosmetology, I love the flexibility of switching up a hairstyle. However, as a sociologist/social scientist, I have focused this text on a deeper issue than just changing your hairstyles. I'm speaking about the psychological problems that have been bestowed upon Black folks sociologically.

4. **Sociologist vs. Psychologist:** If you are wondering about the difference between psychologists and sociologists, know that the two are like cousins. Imagine there is a bank robbery, and detectives call the

"cousins" to the scene to investigate. The psychologist would ask "Why" did the bank-robber rob the bank, while the sociologist, me, would ask "How" did the bank-robber rob the bank. Both disciplines are equally as important as they go hand in hand. However, the psychological discipline focuses on why, and the sociological discipline focuses on how.

5. **Stories of Resistance:** Highlight acts of courage and resilience within the community.

6. **How Colorism Persists:** This part explores the mechanisms that allow colorism to continue, including societal structures and personal behaviors. Understanding these factors empowers us to interrupt and disrupt them through a changed mindset and behavior.

7. **Healing the Black Community:** Finally, we focus on solutions to heal individually and collectively. This section offers practical steps to affirm our African identities, embrace our diversity, and unite as a stronger community.

You will find moments of reflection, understanding, and inspiration as we navigate each part. There is a lot to unpack here, and your cortisol level (the hormone that causes stress) will be raised, and you may experience a huge range of emotions. This is natural. So, as a disclaimer, I would admonish you to grab a cup of tea, take a deep breath, take a long inhale and an even longer exhale. Ground yourself through mindfulness periodically as you begin to read, continue reading, and conclude reading Eternal Black Eye.

This book is not just a compilation of historical facts or sociological theories and frameworks; it's a call to action. It's an invitation to engage thoughtfully with challenging topics and participate actively in healing.

Let us approach this journey with open minds and open hearts. Combining knowledge with compassion can break down the barriers that have separated us and build bridges toward a more unified and empowered community.

THE IMPACT OF THE UNHEALED, SALT-FILLED WOUND

Imagine a deep, painful wound raw and yearning for healing. Instead of nurturing it, someone pours salt into it. The salt not only intensifies the pain but inflames and irritates, preventing proper healing. This relentless re-injury exacerbates suffering and prolongs recovery. The phrase "rubbing salt into the wound" vividly captures this notion of compounded pain.

In the context of our shared history, this metaphorical "salt-filled wound" represents the enduring impact of chattel slavery on African Americans. The initial injuries of slavery were never allowed to heal; instead, they were repeatedly aggravated. Systemic injustices and ongoing oppression have deepened these emotional and psychological wounds, leaving scars on both individuals and the community at large.

CHATTEL SLAVERY AS THE ORIGINAL WOUND

Chattel slavery was not merely a blemish in history it was a deliberate and calculated system of oppression. A blemish may mark the surface of the skin temporarily, but it eventually fades. While a black eye is a huge blemish, that one can use foundation make up to cover up. Society expects that silence of the global majority and that no mention of this crime of humanity would serve as it's cover up.

Slavery, on the other hand, left a wound far deeper than any external mark. It stripped Black people of their humanity, identity, and dignity. Families were torn apart, languages silenced, cultures suppressed, and individuals reduced to mere property.

This system was a trauma, a wound that went beyond physical pain. It fractured ancestral ties, halted cultural continuity, and left an indelible mark an "Eternal Black Eye" on the collective psyche of the enslaved and their descendants. The emotional, psychological, and spiritual scars were profound, much like an untreated wound festering until amputation seemed the only solution. Yet, instead of addressing this pain, society has often chosen to "cut it off" and pretend the trauma never existed. This denial perpetuates harm, compounding what began centuries ago.

Anti-Black racism happens on multiple levels, which serves as more injury that creates this eternal black eye.

Let's look at just a few.

There is medical racism where J. Marion Sims (1813-1884) has been called the "Father of Gynecology" for his revolutionary approach to treating the diseases of women. He experimented on enslaved Black women while using no anesthesia because he declared that Black people could not feel pain. All of this was done in the name of "advancing medicine."

The ideology that Black folks are unable to feel pain has not changed much today. Black patients are less likely to receive pain medication prescriptions from their doctors.

Ask yourself, have you ever been in severe pain that required a "stronger medication," and the doctor dismissed your pain and directed you to "take something over the counter like ibuprofen, and you'll be fine." The notion that Black folks do not feel pain is abhorrent. This is a shared experience for many Black individuals a modern echo of Sims' grotesque practices.

Not only has the system of oppression deemed us to not feel pain, but Black folk's desire for freedom was also pathologized.

Have you heard of the mental illness called Drapetomania?

When enslaved Black folks tried to run away and escape the brutality and harsh conditions they were forced to endure at the hand of their oppressors, they were declared to be crazy, or in the diagnosis of Dr. Samuel Cartwright, who served as "Professor of Diseases of the Negro" in the Medical Department of the University of Louisiana (now Tulane University), diagnosed the desire for enslaved Black folks to run away, as a psychological illness, called Drapetomania.

Cartwright and other early proponents of racial medicine were key players and instrumental in the long process of embedding racist ideologies into medical knowledge education and practice (Willoughby, 2018). As Willoughby notes, these early "experts" shaped a medical framework that viewed Black people as biologically inferior, a lie that has long outlived them.

Today, many resist acknowledging the wickedness of these historical crimes. The upholders of colonial ideologies would rather silence discussions about the atrocities inflicted upon the global majority. But ignoring these truths does not erase them. Instead, it deepens the wounds, creating an eternal black eye that demands reckoning.

THE AFTERMATH

The abolition of slavery didn't heal these wounds. Instead, subsequent systems of oppression Jim Crow laws, redlining, mass incarceration, and cultural stereotyping aggravated them further. These injustices fueled feelings of pain, anger, and hopelessness that persist today.

Instead, healing, the wound remained open, repeatedly aggravated by systems of oppression that followed.

Today, the aftermath of slavery manifests in ways that continue to shape the African American experience:

Internalized Racism: Absorbing harmful stereotypes about one's racial group.

Colourism and Texturism: Valuing lighter skin tones and certain hair textures over others.

Distrust and Division: A legacy of slavery's divide-and-conquer tactics that sowed mistrust within the community.

These effects hinder self-perception, relationships, and unity, perpetuating the cycle of trauma.

A CALL TO ACTION: CONFRONTING THE LEGACY OF OPPRESSION

Understanding our history is vital to reclaiming our future. Too often, history is rewritten, sanitized, or dismissed, as though time alone heals systemic oppression. But the truth is, these systems didn't dismantle themselves, they evolved.

To move forward, we must interrogate history, asking difficult questions:

How were we divided?

Why does colorism persist?

How do we overcome internalized racism and affirm our Blackness?

This journey begins by examining the roots of division and understanding how colonial tactics continue to shape our reality. By confronting these truths, we take the first step toward healing.

Internalized racism is a seldom discussed but critical aspect of systemic oppression. It refers to subconsciously accepting and perpetuating society's racist views, stereotypes, and biases about one's racial group. Consider these examples:

Language: Phrases like "good hair" or "light-skinned privilege" reinforce harmful beauty standards.

Behavior: Preference for Eurocentric products and success markers over culturally affirming alternatives.

Perception: Associating intelligence, professionalism, and beauty with whiteness while devaluing Blackness.

Recognizing these patterns allows us to address and heal the wounds they create.

WHY THIS MATTERS

As a social scientist, I aim to provide tools for collective healing—empowering us to address internalized racism and shift paradigms toward valuing the African Diaspora. Cognitive behavioral frameworks show how thoughts influence feelings and behaviors, creating cycles that either perpetuate or break oppression (Metzger et al., 2021).

To move forward:

Reflect on Personal Experiences: Consider how historical wounds have shaped your perspectives.

Engage in Dialogue: Foster understanding and support through open discussions.

Promote Healing Practices: Celebrate cultural heritage and affirm positive identities.

Let's embark on this journey not with guilt or blame, but with a shared commitment to growth and healing. Acknowledging the unhealed, salt-filled wound is the first courageous step toward mending it. Together, we can transform a legacy of pain into a foundation for strength, resilience, and unity.

In the chapters ahead, we'll explore how internalized racism manifests and, more importantly, how we can overcome it. By uncovering layers of history, understanding their impact, and envisioning a healed future, we move closer to breaking cycles of oppression and achieving collective liberation.

Remember: Healing begins with understanding. Understanding inspires action. And collective action creates lasting change.

1

HISTORICAL CONTEXT OF COLONIALISM

As a Black sociologist, I've spent years studying the origins of colorism and its impact on our communities. The evidence is clear. Colonial powers didn't just enslave bodies, they manipulated minds.

On plantations, European colonizers exploited skin tone differences to create divisions. Lighter-skinned individuals were placed in the house, while darker-skinned individuals were forced into the fields. This artificial hierarchy wasn't random. It was deliberate.

By offering small privileges to lighter-skinned people—better treatment, access to education, and rare chances for freedom—colonizers splintered unity. These calculated moves tore apart families and created tensions that still ripple through generations.

Elders often share stories of these divisions, passed down like cautionary tales. The pain is real. The wounds are deep.

These echoes can today be seen in the disparities of modern times. For example, it has been studied that those who have lighter skin tones are regarded as more capable or professional in their workplace. It seems like the same bias deliberately sowed during the colonial period. That would point out the ways through which such systems of privilege and exclusion survive in more subtle manners that do more harm.

What particularly strikes me in my research is how these manufactured hierarchies became painfully internalized within our communities over time. The psychological impact runs deep - I've interviewed countless community members who share experiences of how skin tone continues to affect everything from social acceptance to job opportunities.

Understanding these colonial roots is crucial as a scholar committed to our community's healing. When we recognize colorism as a deliberate tool of oppression rather than a natural development, we can better work toward dismantling its lingering effects in our lives today.

INTENTIONAL CREATION OF DIVISIONS

Colonial rulers understood that unity among the oppressed could significantly threaten their authority. To prevent this, they meticulously crafted social hierarchies and social stratification that favored lighter-skinned individuals over their darker-skinned counterparts. This strategy was evident in various aspects of daily life:

Social Stratification: Laws and societal norms were established to create clear distinctions between lighter, and darker-skinned Black individuals. For example, implementing the "paper bag test" determined social acceptance based on whether a person's skin was lighter than that of a brown paper bag. Such practices ingrained the notion that lighter skin was more desirable and socially acceptable.

Educational Disparities: Schools often provided better resources and opportunities to lighter-skinned Black students. These disparities created a sense of superiority among those who benefited and feelings of inferiority among those who did not. Educational systems actively reinforced colorism by favoring lighter-skinned individuals in opportunities for advancement.

Employment Practices: Job opportunities were frequently allocated based on skin tone, with lighter-skinned individuals receiving preferential treatment. Employers often held biases that associated lighter skin and straighter hair with intelligence or trustworthiness, deepening economic disparities within the community. Black women have been told that their hair isn't "professional" in work settings. In the context of internalized racial oppression, colorism and hair textures add a dimension to understanding what some Black women may experience and internalize, mainly related to the standards of beauty that they have been excluded from and that are based on white supremacist ideals and Anti-Black racism. Smith, L. L. (2022).

By fostering these divisions, colonial powers effectively weakened the collective strength of the Black community. Internal conflicts and hierarchies made it more challenging for the community to unite against common oppressors, ensuring that these divisions would persist long after colonial rule officially ended. Colonialism didn't just steal our labor—it stole our unity. By sowing division, it ensured that we remained fractured, making resistance nearly impossible. These wounds didn't heal with time; they evolved into systemic barriers that still shape our reality. To move forward, we must first confront how deeply these divisions run and the lasting trauma they've left behind.

Chattel Slavery: Chattel slavery was not merely a system of forced labor; it was a comprehensive assault on the very essence of the African identity. Enslaved Africans were stripped of their cultural heritage, languages, and family bonds, leading to profound psychological and cultural wounds that endure even today.

Psychological Trauma: The relentless dehumanization and brutality of slavery inflicted deep psychological scars. Enslaved people were subjected to physical abuse, sexual exploitation, and constant humiliation. Psychological trauma led to a collective trauma that severely affected their sense of self-worth and identity. Alvarez argues that healing from trauma in a racialized context requires an act of collective, critical resistance whereby educators and researchers reject a White-dominant colonial perspective of trauma because it is pathologizing in several ways. (Alvarez et.al, 2022).

The deliberate severance from cultural identity and imposed inferiority inculcated a deep psychological wound. This trauma has taken on the role of internalized racism over generations, whereby individuals adopt oppressive beliefs about their self-worth and identity. That emotional wound is still going strong today through colorism self-hate, and a general sense of need to assimilate into standards of beauty and behaviors set forth by the Eurocentric. Awareness of these patterns is important in tearing down the lasting impacts of colonialism.

Cultural Suppression: Efforts to erase African cultures were systematic and pervasive. Enslaved individuals were prohibited from practicing their traditional religions, speaking their native languages, and maintaining cultural customs. This cultural erasure disrupted the transmission of heritage and left a void in personal and communal identities.

Family Disruption: Families were routinely torn apart, with spouses, parents, and children being separated and sold to different owners. Family disruptions not only caused immediate emotional devastation but also dismantled the fundamental support structures that are crucial for healthy psychological development.

These psychological and cultural wounds have left an indelible mark on the Black community; they left an eternal black eye. The loss of identity, coupled with the internalization of imposed inferiority, has contributed to ongoing struggles with self-esteem, mental health, and community cohesion.

The "Unhealed, Salt-Filled Wound" as an Enduring Effect

The metaphor of the "unhealed, salt-filled wound" poignantly captures the enduring impact of chattel slavery on the African American community.

Persistent Trauma: The trauma inflicted by slavery did not dissipate with its abolition. Instead, it evolved, embedding itself into the collective consciousness. This persistent trauma manifests in various forms, such as internalized racism and colorism where individuals subconsciously adopt the oppressive standards imposed upon them, which equate to maladaptive behaviors. Maladaptive behaviors in response to racism can include aggression, substance use, and abuse. No wonder there are so many liquor stores in our communities. Nothing is by happenstance.

Intergenerational Impact: Inherited trauma, while the trauma may be indirect as generations pass, the lasting effects directly correlate to the behaviors expressed.

Systemic Oppression: The structures established during colonial times have persisted and adapted over the years. Systemic racism, economic disparities, and social hierarchies continue to reflect the divisions initially created by colonial powers. These enduring systems perpetuate a cycle of pain and suppression, unhealing the wounds.

Contemporary examples abound. For instance, the state of health facilities and administration must be radically made to cater more effectively to Blacks today, just as it was at the beginning continuum of systemic neglect initiated during colonial times. Reports of higher maternal mortality rates among Black women are a further indication that some roots of systemic issues run deep and that they keep rubbing the wound with salt.

Understanding the concept of the "unhealed, salt-filled wound" is crucial for recognizing how deeply entrenched these issues are within the African American community. It highlights the necessity of addressing both historical and contemporary factors that sustain colorism and internalized racism. Acknowledging and confronting these enduring wounds is the first step toward healing and unity in our community.

CONNECTING HISTORY TO PRESENT-DAY REALITIES

As we explore these historical foundations, it becomes evident that the divisions intentionally created by colonial powers have transformed into self-sustaining systems within our community. Born out of a need to control and oppress, these systems now operate with such ingrained efficiency that they perpetuate themselves without conscious intent. Regardless of the intent, the impact is always greater.

The deliberate strategies of colonialism, social hierarchies, economic incentives, and psychological conditioning have become woven into the fabric of society. They influence our attitudes, behaviors, and self-perceptions, making colorism a persistent and pervasive issue. By understanding this historical context, we can better grasp the complexities of colorism and work toward dismantling the harmful structures that continue to divide and weaken us.

LOOKING AHEAD

With this historical foundation established, we can now critically examine how these divisions persist in contemporary society. The chapters ahead will explore the ways internalized racism manifests in both personal relationships and professional spaces, shaping interactions, opportunities, and self-perception. By analyzing these patterns, we can uncover the mechanisms that sustain division and chart a path toward collective healing and empowerment.

The goal is to work toward creating a more unified and empowered African American community. Understanding our past equips us with the knowledge to challenge and change the present. Together, we can heal the unhealed wounds, remove the salt that exacerbates our pain, and foster a future where unity and self-acceptance prevail.

THE UNSPOKEN WOUND: HISTORICAL ROOTS AND INTERNALIZED RACISM

To truly understand where colorism within the African American community comes from, we need to journey back in time to the roots planted during colonialism. Imagine the immense power colonial rulers held, driven by their hunger and greed for wealth and control. They knew unified people could challenge their authority, so they devised ways to divide us.

CHATTEL SLAVERY: INFLICTING DEEP PSYCHOLOGICAL AND CULTURAL WOUNDS

Enslaved Africans were stripped of their languages, cultures, and family bonds. Imagine being torn from everything familiar, with no way to pass down traditions or stories from your ancestors. Chemist and hair care pioneer, Dr. Willie Morrow's 400 Years Without a Comb documentary declares that during our forced migration, colonial powers did not allow us to bring our grooming tools, particularly our comb. This was yet another hit to an already black eye, and to pour more salt into the wound, enslaved women were forced to cover their hair, creating yet another psychological injury that focused on the aesthetic of our tightly coiled hair and natural African features.

The psychological trauma of this colonial game has been effectively played on all Black folks; no one was exempt. Sadly, some of our lighter-skinned Black brothas and sistas have also fallen victim to the colonial deception. The reason that this book was written was to put all these things into perspective. Yes, we Black folk come in myriad shades, from "high yella" to the deepest ebony, like the skin of a sun-kissed, beautiful satin-smooth black plum. However, society has given those members of our community, with lighter complexions, a false sense of security, in that they have gained access to the colonial order of acceptance.

The sad truth is they have not. Their lighter complexion only allows the upholders of colonialism a space to feel "comfortable." This false ideology and perception that lighter-skinned Black folk are more docile and more trustworthy than our darker brothers and sisters, too, is an extreme level of foolishness and psychological trauma that has been self-inflicted by upholders of colonialism and passed on to the community of the global majority, those from the African diaspora. We must realize that we are in the same boat regarding social stratification. In the words of excellent reggae legend Peter Tosh, "I don't care where you come from, as long as you're a Black man, you are an African," rings loud and clear.

THE PLAYGROUND

As a child, hell, even as an adult today, there seems to be a negative connotation associated with being from the African diaspora. Nobody wants to be "African". Even as a child in elementary school, Johnson Elementary School to be exact, it seemed as though no kids wanted to be "just Black".

Kids on the playground would "base on each other," which means hurling the most insulting words without cussing, it is similar to how celebrities have a roasting session. The term "African Booty Scratcher" was high on the list; the kids would laugh and think that this term was hilarious. However, the child being called an African Booty Scratcher was so opposed to being called that…of course, no child wants to be called any kind of booty scratcher, for that matter. However, I think the perceived insult lies in the word African, as though something was wrong with the relation or connotation to the continent of Africa. There was a subconscious disconnection from Africa that was happening to us, even as children.

Everyone always seemed to assert that they were "mixed with Indian," you know… Native American, or the claim was that their great-great-grandmother (whom they had never met, nor have a photo of) was white. I am not saying that they weren't, or that the stories they had been told regarding their genealogy were not true; it just seemed like the kids felt that the assertion that they weren't just Black, was a great thing or a flex that would elevate their social status.

Ironically, perceivably "mixed" bi-racial girls would use their biracial status as a flex too, not in an innocuous way, but in a vindictive way, almost to say, "I'm Black, but at least I'm not that Black." Of course, our biracial brothers and sisters should be proud of both sides of their parental heritage. I just think that it is essential that we remind our children that the depths of our complexions have always been the source of our rejection, and we must love all of us, from the deepest melanin to those of us in between.

As an adult and a social scientist, I now realize that this was yet another way that we Black folks were pre-conditioned to unconsciously seek proximity to whiteness. I do not blame the kids that I grew up with for making these claims; ironically, I was told the same thing about my genealogy. I was always told that my maternal great-grandmother was part Choctaw Indian, and my paternal great-grandfather was Blackfoot Indian. I do not have a reason to not believe it. I can only go off what my family told me to be true. However, for clarity, no one that I know of in my family is a registered Indian (Native American). However, even being tribally registered was skewed at the hands of colonialism, as during the Dawes Act of 1887, several white people bought themselves a card declaring their Native American registration and citizenship for five dollars and have become known as $5 Indians. Of course, that would be a topic of discussion for another book.

Ultimately, we are all mixed with "something," especially since our Black enslaved grandmothers had no consent over their bodies and were subjected to sexual assault and being brutally raped. I do not doubt that these things are true. Only many of us do not have a genetic record of it.

Ironically, there are grown adult Black folks choosing to deny any affiliation to the continent of Africa, saying, "I'm not African." That is so bizarre and disheartening, and many are adamant about it. So much so that they get upset with the very thought of their melanin having any connection to Africa; this trauma is deeply rooted in colonialism and must be undone. In the words of my favorite reggae band, Steel Pulse, "I curse that day; the day they made us slaves… but our history is no more a mystery". I can imagine that someone is probably reading this chapter right now and declaring to the high hills, "I'm not black", all while denouncing any connection to the African diaspora.

There is a deeper psychological issue here. For the individuals with melanin who'd prefer to distance themselves from any connection to Africa, I would admonish them to ask themselves, what is the problem with having a connection to the African diaspora? Especially when you look in the mirror and you have the phenotype. Do you see the colonial deception inflicted by such a thought process? It is like the memory has been stripped and erased from us. But how?

Stokely Carmicheal said, "We MUST RECOGNIZE that black people, whether we are in Durham, North Carolina; San Francisco, California; Jamaica, Trinidad, Brazil, Europe - or on the mother continent, that we are all an African people, we are Africans, there can be no question about that." (The Black Scholar, 1997)

Sadly, the relentless brutality inflicted deep psychological scars. Our ancestors faced unimaginable physical abuse, humiliation, and dehumanization. Such trauma didn't just disappear; it embedded itself into the collective psyche, affecting how we view ourselves even today. Society would prefer that we nestle into comfortable oppression.

This internalization affects behavior in profound ways:

- Self-Perception: We may develop feelings of inferiority, low self-esteem, and/or self-doubt. We may question our intelligence, beauty, or value based on societal standards that favor whiteness. This becomes a silent struggle that many are faced with.

- Behavior Towards Others: Internalized racism can lead to divisiveness within our community. We might project negative stereotypes onto others who share our racial identity, perpetuating cycles of criticism and distrust.

- Life Choices: It may influence decisions regarding education, career paths, relationships, and social circles, often limiting opportunities based on a perceived lack of worth or fear of confirming stereotypes.

- Assimilation Efforts: Some may alter their appearance, speech, or behavior to align more closely with Eurocentric norms, distancing themselves from our cultural heritage to gain acceptance or avoid discrimination. This assimilation provides a pseudo-psychological sense of proximity. Due to this lack of self-esteem and this development of self-hate, the imposter is born, or as described in this text, "the actor."

GOOD HAIR: THE BEAUTY SCHOOL

There's a pervasive bias toward hair textures that are straighter or have looser curls, often viewed as more "manageable" or professional. At some point, every Black person has heard the term "Good Hair." It's not a formal introduction, but it's universally understood. "Good hair" typically refers to hair that is soft with a loose curl pattern, often associated with bi-racial or "mixed" hair. Such hair can be combed and styled with just a little grease and water. On the other hand, tightly coiled hair requires more effort.

Every Black girl who doesn't have what's perceived as "good hair" has likely experienced anxiety about how their hair will look after a swim, especially when surrounded by non-Black friends. Our tightly coiled hair swells up and changes significantly, a stark contrast to its original state. The concern doesn't stem from the hair itself but from society making us feel like our hair isn't "good enough."

While "good" has a clear opposite in "bad," I've never heard anyone say, "Dang, that's some bad hair!" However, the term "nappy" often emerges in these conversations. As a Professor of Cosmetology, I make it a point to ensure my students never use the term "nappy" to describe hair. That word can easily be seen as another form of the "N-word." Hair should be described by its texture and curl pattern, not demeaning labels.

One day, I went to work. I was the night instructor at a cosmetology school and came in early to work. I was at the front desk when a Black woman came in and requested a silk press/ flat iron service. Her hair was natural, unrelaxed, and had no chemical straighteners. Now, the students are randomly selected to service guests so that they can learn to do a variety of clients' hair, which helps equip them for the professional salon world. I make it a point for my students to be able to style my curly hair properly; otherwise, I feel that I am doing them a disservice, mainly since they can easily get typecast from the front desk receptionists/ salon coordinator and be assigned clients whose hair closely matches their own, meaning that the Black girls may only get curly hair clients that requests silk press / flat iron styles and the white girls are more likely to get all the haircut and hair color clients who have straight hair.

Well, this day, the school's salon coordinator called the student to the front desk to pick up her ticket and meet her client. Remember, this was the day shift; my class did not start until evening, and I arrived early. I do not know any of the daytime students, nor do I remember this student's or the client's name, but for the sake of this story, I will refer to the student as "Heather-Anne" and the client as Ms. Maybel.

So, Heather-Anne came to the front desk, swung her blond hair over her shoulder, swiftly grabbed her ticket, and called out "Maybel?" "Yes," said Ms. Maybel, "you can follow me." The salon coordinator looked at me and mouthed, "Maybel, follow me". It was evident that we both felt that Heather-Anne's greeting lacked professionalism and decorum, however, this is why she was in school, to not only learn to do hair, but to learn the salon business and soft skills like customer service. Since we were in the middle of a shift change and there were no daytime instructors readily available, I decided to go to Heather-Anne's station and observe her consultation.

Heather-Anne draped Ms. Maybel with a shampoo cape and proceeded to put her own hair in a ponytail; then she looked at the ticket and looked up at Ms. Maybel and, with an air of disgust, said, "Oohh, your hair is NAPPY, and you want a flat iron?" I saw the shocked look on Ms. Maybel's face, and I immediately intervened. "OH, NO, we don't use the term NAPPY!" Heather-Anne looked shocked and appalled that I had the audacity to correct her. "We always say nappy!" said Heather-Anne. "WE, WHO?" I asked. "Me and the daytime instructors," she said. As I did an instant mental replay of who the daytime instructors were, I realized that none of them were Black.

Now my wheels began to turn, wondering, "Is this the terminology that they are using toward Black clients with tightly coiled hair?" I let Heather-Anne know that using this terminology, NAPPY, was, for one, disrespectful and derogatory toward Ms. Maybel and Me, and secondly, that it was unprofessional as a cosmetologist. Ms. Maybel, an older Black woman who had lived through the Civil Rights era, took a deep sigh and looked so insulted and defeated by this young white girl who addressed her in this manner. At that moment, it felt like Ms. Maybel, and I had taken a time warp back to the 1950s or 60s.

This was a problem that I needed to deal with immediately! Regardless of the student's intent, the impact is always greater. I apologized to Ms. Maybel… all the while, I was thinking, "Oh, hell no! What instructor uses this derogatory term and/

or finds it acceptable for students to say it?" So, I wanted to make this a teachable moment; I then asked Heather-Anne, "What are you trying to convey when you use the term nappy?" She didn't quite understand my line of questioning, so I elaborated, "When you say nappy, what are you trying to describe?" She said, "Her hair is super curly and tangled." I replied, "Okay, so that is a professional way of describing... so, you are referring to her curl pattern and the state of being that the hair is in?" "Yes," Heather-Anne said. I replied, "Well, moving forward, that is how you describe hair; you use professional terms to describe texture and curl patterns." Ms. Maybel interjected, "Yes because you might say that term to another client, someone who is not so forgiving, and you may have a different situation on your hands."

Ms. Maybel thanked me and Heather-Anne but decided she no longer wanted her hair done. As she stood up, she paused, took a deep breath, and with a slight raise of her brow, her head seemed to lower, and she briefly shut her eyes, took a long blink, and subtly shook her head. The nonverbal communication told me she was disheartened and that we've come a long way but still have a long way to go.

Unfortunately, Heather-Anne was more concerned with the fact that she had been corrected than what she was being corrected about. The next day, I was called into the office and informed that Heather-Anne had complained that I corrected her about using the term nappy. I then proclaimed, "I was hired to teach, and I taught this student that it is insulting and unprofessional to describe a client's hair as nappy and that I gave her the proper verbiage. Is this not teaching?" I asked.

With an already made-up mind, the individual stated, "I looked online, to see if Black people felt that it was insulting for someone to call their hair nappy, and the results were 50/50. Fifty percent of Black people think that saying Nappy is offensive, so therefore, the other half of the Black people are unbothered by it!"

"Humm, that's interesting, you took a survey? Perhaps we should do a survey here, on our live guests" I replied. The rationale behind this statement was ludicrous. The topic of concern was not the negative impact that Ms. Maybel had from Heather-Anne's use of this demeaning and unprofessional terminology. Instead, the problem focused on my audacity to correct Heather-Anne's sense of entitlement. Ironically, less than two weeks later, I was informed that I was being laid off due to "budget cuts".

Hair Alteration Practices: The pressure to conform leads many to chemically straighten or alter their natural hair, sometimes causing physical harm or emotional distress.

It is essential to know that Black folks have experienced discrimination, not only due to their skin color but also due to the texture and curl pattern of their hair. This is why people with melanin around the globe are referred to as afro-something. "Afro-American, Afro-Swedes, Afro-Latina," AFRO, AFRO, AFRO! So, it is the Afro that is also bothersome. Have you ever gone to a job interview and wanted to straighten your hair instead of wearing it in its natural curl pattern? I have. I had a huge afro, and I found myself wanting to straighten it before my interview. But why? Could it have been to make the interviewer feel comfortable, or is it because navigating this world with the intersectionality of being Black and a woman requires us to go along to get along? Whatever the reasoning behind it is, it caters to white superiority. Take, for instance, NBA player Allen Iverson, who used to wear his hair braided in cornrows during the 90s; he took a lot of flak for wearing a cultural style. Supervisors on jobs across the U.S. wouldn't allow their Black employees to wear braids, as they deemed it unkempt.

Throughout this book, you will hear me reference the terms texture and curl pattern. Often, people confuse or interchange the two. Here is why: the two go hand in hand. Without providing a long-drawn-out cosmetology lesson, let me explain. The texture of hair is described as "Fine, Medium, and Course." If I were to ask you to select only one of those three textures, that you think relates the closest to a Black person's hair, which texture would you select? Write your answer somewhere, and I will answer that question shortly.

Texture simply means the diameter of the individual hair strand (how fat or skinny the strand is). Imagine a fat boba straw, that would be equivalent to course textured hair, now imagine a KFC straw, that would be equivalent to medium textured hair, finally imagine a skinny red coffee stirrer, that would be equivalent to fine textured hair. Does that make sense?

Now let's get back to that texture question. If you answered that the texture that comes to mind when thinking about a Black person's hair, is course texture. I must tell you that many people would select the course texture as their answer too. But the truth is, that for the hair strand to coiled, the strand must be skinny, making the hair texture…FINE! A great majority of Black people have fine textured hair (a skinny strand). You typically find that Asians and Pacific Islanders have course textured hair (a fat strand like a boba straw)

The reason I brought up texture is because there is a negative connotation with having course-textured hair. However, the connotation is false, as the texture, being the diameter of the individual strand, is not the real problem. Society's real issue is the Afro, and that is the curl pattern that is synonymous with people of melanin, the global majority.

LANGUAGE AND COMMUNICATION

Devaluing African American Vernacular English (AAVE) is the dismissal of Black linguistic heritage, labeling it as inferior or uneducated while ignoring its deep historical and cultural roots. Viewing our natural speech patterns as inferior or uneducated, leading to code-switching or language policing within the community, and devaluing the sentence syntax of those of the Black community. Harvard linguist Professor Sunn M'Cheaux correlates the etymology of words, their pronunciation, and their origins, giving AAVE and Gullah Geechee language its voice and platform while putting to rest that American Standard English is the only way to communicate. There are vernaculars amongst cultures that serve as viable means of communication, such as, in Professor M'Cheaux's words," Blacronysms." IYKYK.

CULTURAL DISSONANCE

Cultural dissonance is the internal conflict that arises when Black identity is measured against Eurocentric standards. After generations of systemic oppression, many have been conditioned to distance themselves from their own heritage—rejecting cultural traditions, music, language, and aesthetics to fit into spaces that were never designed for us. This survival tactic is not assimilation; it's erasure, forcing us to shrink who we are to be deemed acceptable.

STEREOTYPE ENDORSEMENT

These internal conflicts don't just shape personal identity—they reinforce harmful stereotypes, fuel division, and create barriers to collective success.

Believing Negative Stereotypes: Accepting harmful generalizations about laziness, criminality, or lack of intelligence as truths about our community.

Mistrust and Competition: Viewing fellow community members with suspicion or seeing their success as a threat rather than a collective victory.

Imposter Syndrome: Feeling undeserving of achievements or opportunities, leading to self-sabotage or withdrawal from challenging pursuits. Remember, the imposter is "the actor."

Overcompensation: Pushing oneself to extremes to prove worthiness, often at the expense of mental and physical health. This overcompensation causes workplace trauma.

INTERNALIZED RACISM AS AN "UNSPOKEN WOUND" OF COLONIALISM

During colonial times, systemic strategies were employed to dehumanize Black people and elevate whiteness as the standard of humanity.

Psychological Warfare: Our ancestors were subjected to relentless messaging that they were inferior, unintelligent, and unworthy of fundamental rights. This was designed to break spirits and enforce compliance.

The wound remains "unspoken" because discussing internalized racism can be uncomfortable, invoking feelings of shame or denial. Yet, acknowledging its existence is crucial for healing.

CONNECTING HISTORY TO PRESENT-DAY REALITIES

As we reflect on this history, it becomes clear that the divisions intentionally created have transformed into self-sustaining systems within our community. They influence our attitudes, behaviors, and perceptions of ourselves and others.

THE PATH TO UNDERSTANDING AND HEALING

Recognizing internalized racism requires courage and honesty. It's about peeling back layers of societal conditioning to examine beliefs and behaviors that may have been adopted unconsciously. Recognizing internalized racism is just the first step—true healing requires action. It calls for deep self-reflection, a commitment to unlearning harmful conditioning, and the intentional rebuilding of our self-worth, our communities, and our cultural pride.

SELF-REFLECTION:

Question Ingrained Beliefs: Ask ourselves why specific beauty standards, success, or intelligence are held. Are they rooted in genuine personal values or inherited biases?

Acknowledge Feelings: It's okay to feel discomfort, anger, or sadness upon realizing how internalized racism has influenced our lives. These emotions are part of the healing process.

EDUCATION:

Learn Historical Contexts: Understanding the origins of internalized racism provides clarity on how it functions and why it's pervasive.

Explore Cultural Heritage: Delve into African and African American people's rich histories, accomplishments, and contributions to foster pride and connection.

COMMUNITY ENGAGEMENT:

Open Dialogue: Discuss internalized racism with family, friends, and community members to raise awareness and support one another.

Collective Action: Participate in or initiate community programs that celebrate Black culture, promote self-acceptance, and challenge oppressive systems.

CHALLENGING SOCIETAL NORMS:

Reject Eurocentric Standards: Embrace and promote diverse representations of beauty, intelligence, and success within the community.

Advocate for Change: Support policies and practices in schools, workplaces, and media that foster inclusivity and dismantle racist structures.

PERSONAL EMPOWERMENT:

Affirmations and Positive Self-Talk: Replace negative internal narratives with affirming messages acknowledging our worth and capabilities.

Mentorship and Role Models: Seek out and become mentors who exemplify positive identity and counteract harmful stereotypes.

With this perspective, we're better prepared to explore how these divisions manifest today—from our relationships to the professional world. By examining these manifestations, we can identify patterns that perpetuate division and take steps to break them.

The goal is to work toward a more unified and empowered African American community. Understanding our past gives us the tools to challenge and change the present. Together, we can heal these unhealed wounds, remove the salt that exacerbates our pain, and build a future where unity and self-acceptance prevail.

Let's continue this journey with open minds and compassionate hearts, committed to learning, understanding, and transforming our shared experiences into a foundation for healing and strength.

In our journey to understand internalized racism and its effects, it is essential to examine how some individuals begin to adopt behaviors and attitudes that mirror those of historical oppressors. This phenomenon is what I consider "wearing the colonial costume and the actor wanting to wield the whip. "This metaphor powerfully illustrates the complex ways in which the legacy of colonialism continues to influence personal identities and dynamics within our community.

By "wearing the colonial costume," individuals may consciously or unconsciously align themselves with the values, norms, and behaviors of the neocolonial culture that once subjugated their ancestors, having the desire to "wield the whip" themselves. This symbolizes an aspiration to attain the power and privilege of the oppressor's role. This can manifest in various ways:

Embracing Oppressive Ideologies: Adopting beliefs that devalue one's culture while upholding the superiority of the dominant culture.

Exerting Control Within the Community: Seeking positions of authority to impose the same oppressive structures on others in their community.

Distancing from Cultural Roots: Rejecting or minimizing aspects of one's heritage to conform to dominant societal norms.

Some may believe they are improving their social standing or gaining acceptance by adopting these behaviors. However, this often perpetuates the very systems of oppression and division that colonialism established. It reinforces harmful hierarchies and undermines the unity and strength of the community.

IT BE YOUR OWN PEOPLE

Have you ever heard the term "It be your own people"? Well, sadly, the effects of this trauma have caused some of our people, our community members, to become "that person." This person who has internalized racism may very well be a family member or even a colleague. It is not that we don't love them. However, our community member who has internalized racism makes it difficult to find common ground. This is yet another blow that colonialism has delivered to our eyes. This member seems to hold resentment and have difficulty loving themselves, and they make it very clear that "All skin folk ain't kin folk." I am confident in saying that 99% of all Black folk have experienced an encounter with this individual. Ironically, this individual is the person that European Americans, who hold bigotry and biased sentiment, are referring to when they say, *"I have a Black friend."*

Have you ever experienced a situation with law enforcement, perhaps something that should be as simple as a traffic ticket or infraction, and you are met with hostility and discriminatory overtones from the initial officer? Then here comes a Black officer, "whew," you breathe a sigh of relief, only to realize that this individual has internalized racism and begins to treat you worse than the initial officer. Of course, that was just an example; however, this experience is not exclusive to any one profession; it could be anywhere. Only this type of opposition is usually presented by someone who has internalized racism and is in a position of authority in that situation. My point is, living within a system of structural racism, we are very aware that there are upholders of colonialism; however, it is more painful when the upholding comes from someone who has a shared lived experience in America as you. This is the actor!

ADOPTING COLONIAL BEHAVIORS AND THE DESIRE TO EXERT POWER: "THE ACTOR"

Let's investigate a sensitive but crucial aspect of our shared experience—where some individuals within our community begin to adopt behaviors and attitudes reminiscent of historical oppressors. The actor believes that their proximity to Eurocentrism removes the injury sustained culturally and historically (well, at least for themselves); at this point, the actor is no longer dedicated to the overall collective of those who are consciously navigating this system of oppression. At this point, the actor has socially and psychologically severed any binding ties to the Black community. The thought process becomes "every man for himself." However, the actor is willing to unite with others who feel the same way about themselves. It should be noted that the actor will sever any relationship if it means that their proximity to Eurocentrism will be increased.

UNDERSTANDING THE PERSONAL JOURNEY

Imagine a person who, consciously or unconsciously, starts to take on traits of the colonial oppressor. This isn't about assigning blame but about understanding the profound psychological impact of systemic oppression on individuals. For example, some individuals feel the need to alter their appearance, perhaps by straightening their natural hair, using hydroquinone to lighten their skin, or adapting their image to Eurocentrism. As a professional image consultant and cosmetology professor, I think flexibility with your hair styling choices is excellent. However, when the psychology behind the change is to gain proximity to whiteness, this may be where the problem lies. They might adjust their tone inflexion and speech patterns, modulating their natural dialect to sound more like the dominant culture.

This assimilation is often driven by the belief that conforming to these standards will lead to better opportunities, acceptance, or respect.

Concerning adaptation and acquired survival skills, Black folks have learned to "code-switch," as it seemed to be an unspoken requirement of corporate America. Code-switching is the ability to turn on that ridiculous, high-octave telephone voice without missing a beat and turn it off, returning to your natural tone. Unfortunately, we've been forced to do this as we navigate racist institutions, however, the actor's switch seems to have malfunctioned or gotten broken, as they are stuck in this caricature. I have become very conscious and deliberate about not allowing the code to switch on me and speaking very matter of fact in my natural chest voice, as opposed to that higher-pitched, head voice that almost begs for colonial approval and that is intentional.

Some individuals, however, internalize oppressive ideologies. They might begin to uphold beliefs that devalue Black culture, criticizing traditions and practices central to the community's heritage. By elevating white culture as superior, they inadvertently reinforce the same ideologies used to oppress them. Dr. Joy Degruy says that "African Americans have been socialized to be something akin to white racists and that many of us have adopted the attitudes and views of a white, racist America" (Degruy, 2005).

In more extreme cases, individuals may seek authority not to uplift the community but to perpetuate oppressive structures within it. This could involve enforcing rigid hierarchies, discriminating against others based on skin tone or features, or promoting policies that harm rather than help. The desire to wield power in this way often mirrors the tactics used by historical oppressors.

HOW DOES THIS HAPPEN?

The scars of colonialism and chattel slavery didn't simply disappear over time. Instead, they were reinforced, repackaged, and passed down through generations—embedding themselves in our self-perception, our communities, and even our aspirations. This wasn't merely a war on our bodies; it was a calculated attack on the Black mind. A system was put in place to make us question our worth, our beauty, and our very right to exist unapologetically.

The strategies employed by colonial rulers may have been born centuries ago, but their influence still permeates every aspect of our lives today. From the way we evaluate our features to the unconscious biases we carry toward one another, the seeds they planted have taken root and grown into something far more insidious. We have been conditioned to view ourselves through a lens that distorts our true potential, a lens that was never designed to reflect our inherent greatness. And this raises a crucial question: What happens when the chains of oppression are no longer imposed externally but are instead upheld from within?

For generations, the pervasive message has been that whiteness is the gold standard of beauty, intelligence, and success. This idea, deliberately planted in our collective consciousness, has convinced many that if they can simply mirror these ideals, they will be deemed worthy. Some internalize this falsehood so completely that they become the enforcers of the very systems that were meant to oppress us. They measure their worth by how closely they can align with whiteness, believing that they have "arrived," that they have cracked the code, and that the rest of the African diaspora simply needs to do better. This is delusional, the ultimate illusion. Because no matter how much one conforms, assimilation will never equal liberation, it is only another form of control.

Here, we begin to unravel the hidden wound of internalized racism a trauma so deeply ingrained that many don't even recognize it. In the next chapter, we will explore how colonialism didn't just steal our land and freedom; it hijacked our minds, turning us against ourselves. It has shaped how we define success, how we build relationships, and even how we value our worth. But understanding this truth is just the first step. To reclaim our identity, we must challenge the narratives we've inherited and actively work to unlearn the lies that were designed to divide us.

2

THE DEEP SCARS OF INTERNALIZED RACISM

The worst kind of chains are the ones you can't see, the ones that don't need shackles or whips because they live in your head, shaping the way you see yourself and the world around you. For centuries, oppression was brutal and direct chains, beatings, and forced labor. But once slavery was abolished, a new tactic was needed: psychological conditioning. The system no longer had to physically restrain Black people because it had already indoctrinated us to do it ourselves. The plantation evolved into policy, the whip was replaced with social hierarchies, and the master's control was embedded into our self-image.

This is the unspoken wound of internalized racism, a silent but deadly legacy of colonialism that manifests as self-hate, colorism, and a desperate need to assimilate into a society that was never designed to accept us. It is the reason so many of us reject our Blackness, why proximity to whiteness is still seen as a privilege, and why Eurocentric standards continue to dictate beauty, intelligence, and worth.

The lie they told us was simple: If we just played along—if we talked the way they talked, looked the way they looked, and distanced ourselves from our people—we could climb out of oppression. But reality is far more sinister. The pervasive message that whiteness is the standard for beauty, intelligence, and success has pushed generations of us to strive for those ideals. Many have believed that adopting these behaviors would change their narrative, allowing them to overcome the barriers imposed by racism. In this chapter, we will pull back the layers of self-hate, texturism, and assimilation to expose the colonial lie that taught us we were never enough.

This isn't just some abstract theory—it's real life, the kind that flows through the blood of our people. It shapes how we see ourselves, see each other, and understand the world around us. Internalized racism is more than just a personal struggle; it's the mirror image of a system designed to oppress, to intentionally break down our collective sense of who we are.

As a Black social scientist, I've seen firsthand how this poison works. It's slow and sneaky, seeping into our minds, and discombobulating the connections that should hold us together. This is no accident; it's the calculated outcome of a system built to dehumanize us, to take away our power.

The system is crafty. It does not rely on outside forces to maintain their control. It's genius if you can even call it that is in how it turns the oppressed into oppressors. It splits us apart, using skin color, hair texture, the way we talk, and how close we are to whiteness creating a hierarchy within our group that sets us against each other.

These divisions aren't random; they are tools of control put in place to ensure we never truly unite. When we start believing in these oppressive standards, making them our measuring stick for success, we don't just hurt as individuals we become part of the problem, agents of the same system that's been trying to crush us for centuries.

This isn't just about individual pain or figuring out who we are; it's about the calculated destruction of our collective power. Every time we doubt ourselves, every stereotype we believe, every time we pre-judge someone in our community, we feed a system that wants to see us divided. It's a cruel twist: we fight against racism from the outside but unknowingly keep it alive within ourselves and amongst each other.

This is internalized racism in action not just an ill-defined concept, but an actual wound, an eternal black eye, that keeps getting re-injured, stopping us from coming together to heal and rise.

THE EROSION OF SELF: MORE THAN AN IDENTITY CRISIS

When we talk about the suppression of our cultural identity, it's not just academic talk. This is the everyday reality of countless Black folks trying to make it in a world that wants to erase us.

It's the mama straightening her child's hair, not for aesthetics, but to protect them from a society that calls natural Black hair "unprofessional," "messy," or "unkempt." It's the brotha in the boardroom changing his voice and words, avoiding how he talks because he doesn't want to be seen as "unintelligent," "ghetto," or "threatening." The young sista hates her reflection because she's been told her dark skin makes her less beautiful and unworthy.

These actions might seem personal or practical, but they reveal the depth of this psychological war, a colonial legacy that still forces its standards on us.

The signs of this suppression are everywhere and often misunderstood. What might appear like anxiety or depression isn't just a personal struggle; it's the weight of living in a system that constantly tells you you're not good enough. That anxiety comes from continually having to watch how you act, how you talk, and how you look to fit into spaces that were never meant for us. That depression stems from generations of feeling less than others, reinforced by a world that celebrates Eurocentrism while pushing Afrocentrism to the side.

The disconnection runs even deeper, a separation from our roots, a fear of fully embracing our heritage, and a feeling that being ourselves will cost us something. These aren't just passing feelings; they're scars from centuries of colonial rule.

This legacy is so dangerous because it seeps into our psyche without us even knowing. It's passed down within families, where parents and elderly, trying to protect the next generation, teach them how to "fit in" to survive. It's in schools, where textbooks focus on European history and achievements, making Africa a mere footnote. It's in our jobs, the media, and daily interactions, where subtle cues tell us we must sacrifice who we are to be accepted or successful.

These daily attacks on our identity are not random; they're calculated, designed to break our spirits and make us struggle to reclaim the wholeness colonialism tried so hard to take away.

THE CYCLE OF SELF-OPPRESSION

The most heartbreaking part is how this system perpetuates itself. We end up polishing the chains that bind us, thinking we're making progress. Every time we conform to standards rooted in racism – rejecting our natural hair, lightening our complexions, altering our voices, not embracing our uniqueness, and chasing acceptance – we unknowingly strengthen the systems designed to keep us down.

This is no accident. The colonial system was cleverly designed, planting division so deep that it continues to function on its own. We've become both victims and enforcers, trapped in a cycle that is as disturbing as it is sad.

LIBERATION

Let's be honest: every time we choose fitting in over standing together, we play a part in a script written centuries ago. When we judge someone for being "too Black," we perpetuate white supremacist ideologies and do the colonizer's work for them.

This isn't about pointing fingers; it's about waking up. Recognizing how these divisions were created is the first step toward breaking free.

When under any kind of influence, thinking becomes difficult. It's like a seductive grip on the mind, distorting your perception of reality. Many of us are under the influence of the colonial spell, having bought into the lie that if we act a certain way, we'll gain acceptance. The thought evolves into: if we speak differently, tone down our voices, or avoid being too loud, then maybe access will be granted. We've romanticized these ideas, rationalizing false narratives that justify the discrimination and oppression of Black people.

The truth is that the global majority was never included in equality play. As author Kimberly Jones said in How We Can Win,

"They are lucky that what Black people are looking for is equality and not revenge" (Jones, 2022).

Have you ever been in a public space with a group of Black folks, where everyone is talking, laughing, and enjoying themselves? Naturally, there will be moments of "cooperative overlap," where people speak at the same time. It may seem chaotic to outsiders, but to us, it's a natural form of connection. It's an invitation to participate in the conversation.

Yet, society demands we self-regulate to avoid making others uncomfortable. What troubles me is when I hear another Black person say, "This is why they don't like us!" (referring to those upholding colonialism). That statement doesn't hold up. When did they ever truly like us? History shows they didn't. We must break free from this mental stronghold.

CREATING SPACES OF RESISTANCE

To heal, we need spaces where we can resist colonial conditioning together. These aren't just safe spaces; they are places for reclaiming our culture. In these spaces, we:

Unlearn colonial thinking: Identifying and discarding the internalized stories that hold us back, we stop measuring success by Western standards.

Rebuild our collective worth: We restore pride in our shared history and identity.

Strengthen our bonds: We unite against the forces that divide us.

THE POWER OF CRITICAL CONSCIOUSNESS

Education is freedom. Understanding how colonial systems shaped our thinking gives us the tools to dismantle them. This isn't about historical lessons; it's about mental liberation. As Paulo Freire taught, developing "critical consciousness" allows us to recognize oppression and fight back strategically. Critical consciousness refers to the ability to analyze, navigate, and challenge the social forces shaping our lives (Seider et al., 2017).

THE COLONIAL COSTUME

Many of us wear the "colonial costume" – behaviours, mindsets, and appearances adopted to navigate a system that rejects us. Whether changing our hair, voice, or posture, the colonial costume promises acceptance but only delivers exhaustion and disconnection from our true selves. I'll discuss the colonial costume further in Chapter 4.

THE PRICE OF THE COSTUME

Wearing this costume comes at a high cost:

We reject our heritage: We give up cultural practices for a false sense of belonging.

We police our own: We enforce colonial standards on other Black people.

We internalize stereotypes: We reinforce harmful ideas about ourselves and our communities.

No matter how much we try to fit in, we'll never truly be accepted in a system designed to exclude us.

THE REVOLUTIONARY ACT OF HEALING

DISMANTLING INTERNALIZED RACISM

Healing from internalized racism is not passive; it's a radical, revolutionary act of reclaiming what colonialism stole from us. Healing starts with intentionally rejecting colonial beauty standards. For centuries, European ideals of beauty have been promoted as the epitome, while African features have been demonized, making Black people feel that their natural features – broad noses, full lips, tight curls, and deep skin tones – are less than.

To change this, we must celebrate our natural beauty unapologetically. This is about shifting the narrative, asserting that Blackness, in all its forms, is beautiful, powerful, and worthy of praise. When we embrace styles that honour our natural features – whether it's an afro, braids, locs, or a cultural head wrap – we reclaim our bodies as expressions of our culture and history, rejecting the shame imposed by colonialism.

Claiming space for authenticity is a crucial step in this journey. In a world that pressures us to conform to European norms, showing up as our full selves is an act of power and empowerment. This means speaking in our natural voices – whether AAVE, Patois, or other culturally rooted languages – without fear of being labelled "ignorant" or "unintelligent." It means refusing to shrink or water down our identities to make others comfortable. We no longer need to dim our light; it's time to shine and let our brilliance radiate.

By doing so, we challenge the systems that punish authenticity and redefine what it means to be "professional" or "acceptable." I have no interest in gaining acceptance from those who do not want me. When we show up as our true selves, we send a message, especially to younger generations: they are enough as they are. This collective authenticity disrupts the oppressive norms that thrive on conformity and silence.

Lastly, healing requires us to honour and revive cultural practices that colonialism sought to eradicate. This is more than just reminiscing about traditions; it's about actively bringing them into our daily lives and communities. Whether it's practising ancestral customs, teaching indigenous languages, or cooking foods tied to our roots, these acts reconnect us to the histories colonial systems tried to erase.

Honoring cultural practices is not just about the past; it's about using these traditions as a source of strength, pride, and identity in the present. By intentionally celebrating Kwanzaa, teaching our children to braid hair in traditional styles, or dancing to rhythms from the African diaspora, we resist the erasure of our culture. These acts of restoration are revolutionary because they rebuild the cultural foundations colonialism attempted to destroy, reminding us of our resilience, creativity, and collective power.

Together, these intentional acts of rejecting imposed beauty standards, embracing our authenticity, and reviving our cultural practices lay the foundation for revolutionary healing. This journey is not just about individual liberation; it's about creating a legacy of resistance, pride, and wholeness for generations to come.

BUILDING COLLECTIVE STRENGTH

Our power lies in unity, a truth that history has consistently shown. From the shackles of colonialism to the persistent systems of oppression today, the strength of our communities has been tested. Yet, it is in our solidarity and our ability to support one another's authentic expression and challenge the biases that divide us that we begin to restore what was once broken.

In sharing our stories, challenging colorism, and celebrating our culture, we rebuild the solidarity necessary to dismantle systemic racism. These are not just abstract actions; they are a direct challenge to the white power structures that have sought to erase or diminish our identities for centuries. The resilience we show in these everyday acts of resistance contributes to a larger movement, a movement that has deep roots in the historical struggle for dignity and liberation.

A CALL TO ACTION: THE WORK AHEAD

Healing is not a passive act; it is a revolutionary process. It requires us to confront the deep wounds inflicted by centuries of colonization and internalized racism. These wounds are not always visible, but they shape our lives, our communities, and the very institutions we rely on. In addressing these truths, we are tasked with more than just acknowledging the pain; we are called to actively undo the harm.

This work is multi-layered. It begins with an inward look a personal reckoning with the internalized racism that has been cultivated in us through generations of oppression. But it cannot stop there. True liberation demands that we extend our efforts outward, toward the communities and institutions that perpetuate these biases.

CONFRONTING INTERNALIZED RACISM WITHIN

To begin this journey, we must first look inward and acknowledge the internalized racism that often lurks unnoticed within us. This is the subtle, insidious form of racism that can manifest in how we view ourselves, our bodies, and our communities. Whether it's favoring lighter skin, judging natural hair, or feeling the need to conform to certain ways of speaking, these biases are born of long-standing colonial structures designed to divide and diminish.

But recognizing these biases is only the beginning. Dismantling them requires courage and honesty and an ability to face the ways we have unknowingly upheld systems of oppression. Yet, this process of self-healing is not just personal. It is deeply connected to our broader community. As individuals heal, so too does the collective. This work is intergenerational, what we do now paves the way for future generations to exist unapologetically in their full, beautiful selves.

CHALLENGING INSTITUTIONS

Healing also requires us to confront the systems that perpetuate oppression. It's not enough to simply acknowledge internalized racism; we must challenge the very institutions that sustain these harmful narratives. Institutions, whether educational, corporate, or governmentally, often uphold policies that disrespect or marginalize our cultural authenticity.

The need for change is clear. We must demand workplaces where cultural expressions, like natural hair and traditional attire, are respected and celebrated. We must advocate for educational systems that honor the contributions of the African diaspora, providing a more accurate and inclusive view of history. And, perhaps most urgently, we must hold the media accountable for perpetuating harmful stereotypes that continue to shape public perception.

This is not the work of an individual but of a collective community standing together to tear down the structures that have long kept us divided. As we challenge these systems, we must also be prepared to replace them with ones that affirm and uplift our humanity.

CREATING AFFIRMING SPACES

To heal, we need more than just policy changes. We need spaces that nurture and affirm our identities. These spaces, whether at home, in school, at work, or in our neighborhoods must be intentionally created to allow us to be our full, unapologetic selves. They are places where we don't shrink to fit in or compromise to feel accepted. In these spaces, cultural pride is celebrated, traditions are preserved, and connections between generations are strengthened.

Affirming spaces are more than just safe havens from the outside world. They are incubators for empowerment and resistance, where the seeds of self-love and solidarity are planted. These spaces allow us to reclaim the aspects of ourselves that colonial systems have tried to erase. When we build these spaces, we not only nurture our healing but also lay the foundation for a future where cultural expressions are celebrated, not marginalized.

SUPPORTING EACH OTHER

At the heart of healing is community. It is through shared resources, mutual validation, and collective care that we begin to repair the damage done by generations of oppression. This is a call for solidarity acts of care that range from addressing colorism within families to celebrating cultural milestones together. In each of these moments, we strengthen the bonds that hold us together, breaking the cycles of oppression that have long kept us apart.

This solidarity is not just about offering support in times of need; it is about holding each other accountable. Not in a way that judges, but in a spirit of love and shared commitment to growth. When we hold each other up, when we cheer each other on, when we challenge one another to be better, we are engaged in a collective act of healing.

BUILDING THE FUTURE TOGETHER

Healing is not a destination; it is a journey. It is a journey that requires patience, persistence, and love. The work we do now confronting our biases, challenging oppressive institutions, and supporting each other will lay the groundwork for a world where we can thrive unapologetically.

This work is not just for us; it is for the generations that follow. It is about creating a world where our children do not have to struggle with the same wounds we have inherited. It is about rebuilding what was stolen from us, dismantling the systems that were imposed upon us, and creating the conditions for future generations to flourish.

THE FUTURE WE DESERVE

Imagine a world where Black children grow up never questioning their beauty, where they see their natural features celebrated and their authentic voices valued. Picture a generation that moves through the world with confidence, free from the weight of self-doubt or societal judgment. These children will know in their hearts, that their identity is their strength, their culture, their foundation, and that their future is limitless.

This is the future we are fighting for, a future where the mental chains of colonialism are broken, and the resilience of our ancestors is honored in every facet of our lives. It is a future where we are no longer judged by the standards of a system designed to oppress us. Instead, we define our worth, rooted firmly in the richness of our culture and the brilliance of our collective spirit.

THE REVOLUTION OF SELF-LOVE

As James Baldwin once said,

"It took many years of vomiting up all the filth I'd been taught about myself and half-believed before I could walk on the earth as though I had a right to be here."

This, too, is our work to reject the colonial scripts that have long told us we are less than, and to reclaim our right to exist as we are. Recognizing internalized racism is the first step, but recognition alone is not enough. We cannot simply identify the wound; we must begin the process of healing.

Healing is not just personal, it is revolutionary. Every act of self-love, every moment of cultural pride, and every time we affirm our worth is a direct challenge to the system that tried to divide and oppress us. For too long, we have been told that assimilation is the key to survival. To thrive, we must mimic the ideals of a system that was never designed for our success.

But we are not here to conform to any of the afore mention standards. We are the blueprint. Our culture, our resilience, and our brilliance stand on their own. There is no higher standard to reach when we are the standard. That statement is one of empowerment to our psyche.

The fight against oppression is not just fought in the streets; it is fought in our minds, in our homes, and in the way we teach our children to see themselves. It is a battle for our self-worth. So, how do we rebuild what was stolen from us?

The answer lies in the revolution that begins in our minds—a revolution of self-love, self-worth, and self-determination. This is where healing begins, and this is where our power resides. Asé.

3

A SYSTEM DESIGNED FOR SUBJUGATION

Oppression didn't end with the physical chains of slavery it was far more insidious than that. Colonialism's true aim was not merely to control our bodies but to invade our minds, to turn us into complicit participants in our subjugation. Even in the absence of a whip, the colonial master's influence continued to dictate our lives. This was psychological warfare at its finest, a cunning system of control designed to fracture our collective strength.

The colonizers knew that if they could divide us, they could control us indefinitely. So, they set about manipulating every social, economic, and political structure, rewarding proximity to whiteness and embedding hierarchies that turned us against each other. The closer one was to Eurocentric ideals whether in skin tone, education, or cultural assimilation—the more privilege one was granted. Yet, it was never enough for true equality. It was enough to create friction, enough to encourage us to turn against our people. The worst part? It worked.

But this system wasn't about preference it was about power. It was about stripping us of our collective strength so thoroughly that, even after colonialism "ended," the structures of subjugation would continue to perpetuate themselves. The power of the colonizer once imposed externally, was internalized, shaping our communities long after the flags were lowered, and colonial forces withdrew.

This chapter aims to expose the mechanisms of this deceit the social stratifications, the internalized oppression, and the relentless effort to make us believe that assimilation was the key to survival. But compliance was never meant to set us free. This chapter will discuss group-differentiated vulnerability; a labor division that was also a divisive tactic.

THE PSYCHOLOGICAL DIVIDE

During the times of chattel slavery, there existed a distinct division of labor that shaped two separate groups of enslaved people. Those who worked in the fields were labelled "field negroes," subjected to grueling labor under the watchful eyes of the enslavers. Meanwhile, those who worked closer in proximity to the "massa" in the house were given slightly better conditions, better food, and better clothing. These individuals were called "house negroes" or, in a more derisive twist, "house knee-grows."

This distinction was more than just a difference in labor; it was a psychological trap designed to create a sense of superiority in the house negro. The small privileges, often superficial, were enough to breed division and foster resentment between the two groups. They were not offered freedom or equality but a false sense of power, a delusion that their proximity to these enslavers, made them superior to their fellow enslaved people. It was a calculated play, a mechanism of control that worked to fracture the enslaved community from within.

In one of Malcolm X's last speeches, he says, *"There are two types of Negroes in this country. There's the bourgeois type who closes his eyes to his people's condition and is satisfied with token solutions. He's in the minority. He's a handful. He's usually the handpicked Negro who benefits from token integration. But the masses of Black people who suffer the brunt of brutality and the conditions that exist in this country are represented by the leadership of the Honorable Elijah Muhammad."*

—Malcolm X,

Malcolm X's words in his later speeches, where he distinguished between the bourgeois "token" Negroes and the rest of the Black community suffering under systemic brutality, illustrating this divide: The separation of house knee-grows and field negros during chattel slavery were predicated on the division of labor. However, colorism became a huge factor. Fast forward to the 21st century, colorism is still a huge factor; however, it is not the only factor.

Some may declare that the evolution of the modern-day "house knee-grow" ideology can result from one's social and economic status. There is the working-class vs the bourgeoise, then you have the petite bourgeoisie, a social class between the middle and lower classes. Ironically, in the Black community, the term "Boozgie" is one that young folk use loosely; it is to reference that someone is acting in a presumptuous way and that they think that they are better than, or "uppity." So, out of the term petite bourgeoisie is where the terms petty and bougie (boozgie) are derived. We must dismantle this thinking and become unified.

As we analyze the legacies of these divisions, it becomes clear: the social and psychological separations that began in the days of slavery have evolved but persist today. Colorism, economic class, and the continuing marginalization of Black communities feed into this ongoing cycle of division. The "house knee-grow" effect, a term that once described labor division, now extends into class and social strata, where the light-skinned are often privileged over the dark-skinned, where those who assimilate into Eurocentric ideals feel superior to those who resist. This division persists, and its roots lie in the colonial construction of power and control.

In chapter one, you read about "the actor" and their desire to "wield the whip." Well, today, we are no longer physically enslaved on a plantation, forced to labor in the field or the massa's house. However, the actor has acquired a false sense of superiority in his psyche, "the house knee-grow effect." In Bob Marley's Redemption song, he said, "Emancipate yourself from mental slavery; none but ourselves can free our minds"! We must remove the chains from our brains.

Group differentiated vulnerability and the house knee-grow effect created a self-sustaining cycle of trauma. As communities fractured under the weight of these imposed hierarchies, divisions became deeply ingrained, perpetuating the very systems of oppression long after the colonial powers had formally departed. The alignment with whiteness was not just incentivized but also normalized, embedding ideas of inferiority and superiority that continue to shape social dynamics, self-perception, and communal relationships. By now, as you read, you are probably shaking your head, saying, "WOW, colonialism did a number on us"!

PARTICIPATION IN ONE'S OWN SUBJUGATION

One of colonialism's most insidious elements was its ability to force the oppressed to perpetuate their subjugation. It was not just through brute force but through a calculated combination of psychological conditioning and the strategic reward of compliance. This system created social hierarchies that valued lighter skin, Eurocentric features, and Western practices rewarding those who conformed to colonial ideals and punishing those who resisted.

This incentive structure led to the internalized racism we still battle today. Many Black people, encouraged by the system, internalized these values, believing that success required conformity to a Eurocentric ideal. Over time, this system cultivated divisions within communities, sowing mistrust and competition where there could have been unity.

It's critical to understand that the alignment with whiteness was not a passive choice, it was an active reward system, a constant reminder that the road to success lay in turning away from one's heritage and culture. As people conformed, they gained minor rewards, such as access to education, better jobs, and social acceptance. But the promise of full equality was always a mirage, an illusion designed to keep us striving, divided, and ultimately unfulfilled.

Examples of this manipulation include the persistent privileging of lighter skin (colorism) and the devaluation of African languages, religions, and traditions. Scholars like Frantz Fanon in Black Skin, White Masks, and Ngũgũ wa Thiong'o in Decolonizing the Mind have extensively explored the psychological and cultural dimensions of this oppression, offering critical insights into its mechanisms. Works like Audre Lorde's Sister Outsider and Bell Hooks Ain't I a Woman further explore the intersections of internalized oppression and systemic racism.

Understanding these mechanisms' intentional and strategic nature empowers us to address their lasting impacts.

Seeing this widespread manipulation for what it truly is, a tactic designed to foster division and self-doubt, we can take the crucial first step to breaking free.

We can reclaim our personal and collective identities with renewed confidence and unity!

THE LOOKING GLASS SELF: SHAPING IDENTITY

The concept of the "Looking Glass Self," proposed by sociologist Charles Horton Cooley, is key to understanding how colonialism shaped our collective self-image. According to this framework, individuals form their identities based on how they believe others perceive them. As colonized people, we were taught to see ourselves through the eyes of the colonizers, who devalued our cultures, our skin, and our very existence.

This process of internalized oppression is evident when we fail to see the beauty in our heritage. Our children must be taught to love their skin, their hair, and their culture because if we don't, they will grow up believing the colonial lie that they are somehow less than others. This is why we must break the cycle of internalized hatred and teach the next generation to see themselves as beautiful and worthy.

The systems of division and control put in place during colonialism did not disappear with the end of formal colonial rule. They have been passed down through generations, embedded within the structures of society and internalized by the very people they sought to subjugate. To truly heal, we must understand these mechanisms and recognize how they have shaped our identities, our communities, and our lives.

By acknowledging the psychological, social, and economic structures that continue to perpetuate our subjugation, we can begin the difficult but necessary work of dismantling them. We must reclaim our sense of unity and pride, not based on proximity to whiteness but on the richness of our own culture and history. Only then can we begin the long journey toward collective healing and self-determination.

MODERN MANIFESTATIONS OF COLONIAL STRATEGIES

The craftiness of colonial oppression lies not merely in its immediate effectiveness but in its striking resilience. The strategies devised centuries ago were not designed to vanish upon the withdrawal of colonial powers; they were constructed to persist, embedding themselves deeply into the societal structures, cultural norms, and individual psyches of the colonized. Today, these mechanisms continue to shape behavior, perceptions, and identities. This is no accident. The endurance of colonial strategies speaks to their calculated nature, ensuring that the very systems of control would outlast the colonizers' physical presence and continue to operate independently.

Colonial strategies were multifaceted, targeting every aspect of life economic structures, educational systems, media narratives, and interpersonal dynamics. One of the most insidious legacies of colonialism was the creation of a social order based on proximity to whiteness. These hierarchies, initially designed to subjugate, persist today, sustaining divisions along racial lines that continue to shape how people are treated and how they treat each other. Similarly, the economic disparities engineered during colonial times have proven exceptionally enduring. The extraction of wealth and resources from colonized lands and their concentration in the hands of the colonizers created a legacy of poverty and underdevelopment in many formerly colonized nations. These economic divides are not merely historical artefacts; they continue to echo through the present, as access to education, employment, and upward mobility often remain governed by color and perceived cultural assimilation. False Hope of Integration: By offering minor privileges to those who conformed, colonial powers fostered a belief that greater alignment with whiteness would result in complete acceptance.

This illusion kept individuals striving for approval that would never come. Dr. Martin Luther King said, "I'm afraid that I integrated my people into a burning house"!

Education and media, too, play pivotal roles in maintaining these colonial structures. Curricula that prioritize European history and achievements over those of other cultures reinforce the narrative of white superiority. Media representations that glorify Eurocentric standards of beauty and success further entrench these ideals. These messages are so pervasive and ubiquitous that they often go unquestioned, becoming part of the very fabric of society. When we internalize these standards, we don't even notice how they subtly shape our aspirations, our identities, and our perceptions of what is achievable.

Some may argue that "the system is broken." But I believe the system is not broken; it works precisely as intended. The endurance of these colonial strategies is not accidental, it is by design. By embedding themselves into the everyday lives of the oppressed, these systems ensured they would be self-sustaining. They are upheld not just by external forces but by the very people they were designed to control. This is the true craftiness of colonial oppression: it creates a cycle where the oppressed unwittingly perpetuate their subjugation. The systems that oppressed us were designed to endure, and so they do often without us realizing their origins.

Recognizing the endurance of these systems is essential for dismantling their influence. To break free, we must first understand their historical roots and critically examine how they manifest in present-day systems and behaviors. Only then can we begin to deconstruct them and build a more equitable future. To be against racism is no longer enough; we must actively disrupt it at every level.

This disruption begins with an honest reckoning with how colonial legacies manifest in our lives today:

Internalized Racism: The legacy of colonial conditioning often manifests as self-doubt and devaluation within marginalized communities. Individuals may unconsciously adopt Eurocentric standards, perpetuating the very systems that oppressed them.

Colorism and Texturism: These hierarchies, established during colonialism, persist within our communities, determining how beauty, intelligence, and worth are perceived. Lighter skin and straighter hair remain symbols of status, both inside and outside the community.

Systemic Inequalities: Economic and social disparities, born out of colonial exploitation, are reinforced by modern systems that continue to echo the same biases, ensuring that the privileged remain so, and the marginalized remain voiceless.

IMPACT ON SELF-IMAGE AND RELATIONSHIPS

The psychological toll of colonial oppression extends far beyond the individual. It permeates relationships, shaping how we view ourselves, our families, and our communities. Colonialism was never just about land and resources; it was a calculated strategy aimed at controlling minds and manipulating how Black people viewed themselves, their worth, and their connections to each other. The damage caused by these tactics fractured relationships, cultivated mistrust, and undermined the collective power that could have challenged the system.

These divisions, once fostered, spread throughout communities. By placing whiteness at the pinnacle of beauty, intelligence, and social value, colonialism ensured that Black people would view one another as competitors rather than allies. Proximity to whiteness became a form of currency, social capital, a currency that came at the expense of cultural identity and communal unity. The result was an "us versus them" mentality that continues to divide Black people, encouraging a constant race for limited opportunities and social acceptance.

But the damage was not only social it was deeply psychological:

Identity Conflicts: Many of us grapple with feelings of inadequacy, shame, and self-doubt. We measure ourselves against Eurocentric ideals, questioning our worth, our beauty, and our intelligence based on standards that were never designed for us.

Family Divides: Preferences for lighter skin and "good hair" create tensions within our own families, damaging self-esteem and perpetuating harmful ideologies.

Community Fragmentation: The colonial hierarchies designed to divide us remain embedded in our communities. This fragmentation makes unity and solidarity harder to achieve, allowing external forces to continue exploiting our divisions.

But here's the truth: we were never meant to thrive under these conditions. The system was never built for us to flourish. It was designed to keep us divided, disempowered, and disconnected from our roots. And that is why recognizing internalized racism is just the beginning of the journey. To heal, we must actively resist the systems that seek to break us.

The challenge, however, is breaking free and unlearning centuries of psychological conditioning that have kept us mentally captive. But make no mistake: healing is revolutionary. Choosing to love ourselves, to uplift one another, and to reject the colonizer's standards is an act of defiance, a powerful assertion of our humanity and our worth.

So, what does resistance look like in real-time? How do we dismantle the systems that were carefully constructed to keep us divided? In the next chapter, we move beyond awareness and into action. We'll explore how to reclaim our narratives, redefine our identities, and build unbreakable solidarity within our communities. It's time to take back control not just of our futures, but of our pasts. It's time to heal together.

4

ASSIMILATION AS A TOOL OF OPPRESSION

They told us our skin was too dark, our hair too coarse, our dialect too unrefined. They convinced us that everything about us was a flaw. And, for centuries, we believed them.

Colonial rulers understood that true power lay not just in physical domination, but in controlling the mind. The legacy of colonial oppression has left behind an insidious belief: proximity to whiteness offers safety, power, and acceptance. This was no accident. It was a deliberate construct, meticulously cultivated by colonial systems to sustain control long after their physical presence waned.

By creating a hierarchy that rewarded lighter skin tones and European features, colonial powers planted seeds of division within Black communities' seeds that grew into deeply entrenched self-loathing. They knew that if we saw ourselves as inferior, we would police each other, suppress our greatness, and uphold their power structure.

But here's the truth they don't want us to realize: our Blackness is not a burden; it is power. For too long, we have conformed, straightening our hair, softening our voices, and diluting our truth to make ourselves palatable to a society that was never meant to accept us. We are not here to be accepted. We are here to reclaim what was stolen.

In this chapter, we take back what was stripped from us. We dismantle the myths, reject the Eurocentric gaze, and step into the fullness of our identity, without apology, hesitation, or seeking permission. The greatest rebellion against oppression is to love ourselves completely.

THE COLONIAL COSTUME

The "colonial costume" is a sociological framework that I created to accurately describe and identify a set of behaviors and characteristics that one takes one takes on, as a means of gaining acceptance or proximity to Eurocentrism. This is a metaphor for how individuals, consciously or unconsciously, internalize and perpetuate the hierarchies imposed by colonial powers. It symbolizes the pressure to conform to the mold set by the oppressors denying authentic cultural expressions deemed "too Black."

For some, survival meant distancing themselves from Black identity and internalizing ideologies that devalued their existence. Consider the example of a young woman in the early 20th century who aspired to work as a domestic in a white household. If she had lighter skin or straighter hair, she might have been chosen over darker-skinned peers. This reinforced the belief that aligning with Eurocentric standards would bring rewards, while darker-skinned individuals faced not only external discrimination but also internalized feelings of inferiority.

These dynamics didn't just affect workplaces or social opportunities, they seeped into families and communities. Children grew up hearing negative comments about their complexion. These seemingly harmless remarks carried the weight of history engineered to divide, fostering insecurities that reverberated through generations.

By humanizing the legacy of these hierarchies, we begin to understand how deeply rooted colorism is. Recognizing this allows us to reclaim and celebrate the fullness of Black identity.

THE "REGULAR" BLACK FOLKS

The invitation to wear the colonial costume is extended by the upholders of colonialism, making an individual feel as though they have intellectually superseded their fellow Black peers. Sadly, this is a subtle yet devastating blow that adds to the proverbial eternal black eye. Even more painful is when Black individuals themselves, unwittingly or not, buy into this colonial narrative and become fully vested in its perpetuation.

I recall a Zoom session I attended, where the facilitator asked everyone to introduce themselves and share something interesting, they had overcome. When it was my turn, I shared a fun, albeit non-extraordinary, anecdote about appearing on a TV game show, where our team did not win. I spoke also about overcoming the societal pressure for approval. Given that all of us in the session had advanced degrees, sharing such personal stories didn't seem out of the ordinary. Some folks talked about their pets, while others revealed their love for thrilling adventures like skydiving and deep-sea fishing.

But then Kayla spoke up. For the sake of anonymity, I will refer to her as Kayla. I was instantly pleased to see another Black woman in the session. The Zoom group was quite diverse, with about 12 people, five of whom were Black, so it felt reassuring to know we had good representation.

The facilitator called on Kayla. She introduced herself,

"Hi, I'm Kayla; I have 3 children, a wonderful husband, 2 dogs, and a cat."

I thought to myself, "How nice. But then, there was a long, awkward pause, as if she was deep in thought. I assumed she was done, but then she said,

"Ummm, I went to predominantly white schools all my life."

I was slightly puzzled but let it go. Then came the bombshell.

"I've always been very smart," she continued.

"And I've overcome being a smart Black girl who didn't fit in with the Regular Black people."

I was thinking, WTF.

At that moment, I couldn't believe what I had just heard. "Regular Black people?" I thought to myself, blinking in disbelief. I had to gather myself, knowing that I didn't have a poker face, and my expressions revealed everything. I paused for a moment, composed myself, and then it clicked. Kayla was wearing the colonial costume.

She went on.

"Since I was so smart, the regular Black kids didn't want to hang around me, so all my friends were white."

My hand went over my face, and I shook my head. The other participants seemed to feed into her narrative, coddling her with comments like,

"Well, you are in a safe space here; thank you for sharing your wonderful story."

But I couldn't let this slide, for I knew I couldn't contribute to the colonial lie that somehow some Black people are "better" than others and the notion that there were some mystical knee-grows that were smarter than everyone else and that the rest of us knee-grows were "regular Black people"! There was no such thing as the "regular Black people" she was referring to.

So, I raised my hand on Zoom (of course, my hand icon is black, as I feel strange keeping that yellow hand icon that is automatically set to phones and computers, as it is a subtle but notable symbol rooted in racism, but don't get me started). That is a whole other story! The facilitator called upon me. "Toshua, you have your hand up?"

"Yes, I have a question for Kayla."

She responded,

"Yes?"

I proceeded.

"You mentioned that you were smart all your life and that you didn't fit in with 'regular Black people.' I've never heard of that term before, so I'd like to ask for some clarity. What do you mean by 'regular Black people' and what qualifies them as such?"

There was an uncomfortable silence, and Kayla began blinking rapidly, stammering. Her nervousness reminded me of a cartoon character, Barney Rubble from The Flintstones. She nervously muttered,

"Umm, umm... I shouldn't have said 'regular Black people'... I meant, uh, I was in AP classes, and I was talking about the Black kids who were in other classes because all the kids in my class were white."

She continued, her tone becoming defensive.

"All the other kids saw me as 'Ms. Smarty Pants' and they felt like I thought I was better than them."

There it was. This was the persona Kayla had acquired the "token" Black person, the one who had bought into the colonial narrative that somehow being different from other Black people made her superior. I knew that this was her position, and she proudly tried to sell it to everyone on the Zoom call.

But not today.

I felt it was necessary to ask her to reflect on that statement, to hold a mirror to the internalized racism that had shaped her perspective. I felt a sense of sadness for her. As a child, I understood how her actions may have been rooted in survival, but as an adult, she needed to see how the colonial lie had deeply affected her. I hoped that, with time, she could gain the awareness to burn that colonial costume and never wear it again.

HOW DID THIS HAPPEN?

It was an ordinary conversation, yet her words struck me with the force of centuries of history: "I'm not like those Black folks." I knew exactly how she had come to believe this, and my heart sank as I recognized the shadow of a deeply ingrained ideology that society has perpetuated for centuries. The roots of this thought process extend far back in history, shaped by pseudoscience, colonialism, and systemic dehumanization.

This ideology, which upholds white supremacy and Black inferiority, can be traced to the 18th century and the work of Swedish scientist Carl Linnaeus who coined the term "Homo Sapiens". Known as the father of modern taxonomy, Linnaeus categorized humans into four "varieties" based on continent and color. This was no innocent act of scientific classification. Instead, it laid the foundation for "scientific" racism and colonial ideologies.

THE BIRTH OF DEHUMANIZATION

At the bottom of Linnaeus's hierarchy, he placed the African variety, referred to as *after* (later *africanus*), with dehumanizing descriptors. Africans were characterized as "phlegmatic" (relaxed and peaceful), "loose" (calm), and bearing "black frizzled hair" alongside "smooth, silky skin." But these seemingly neutral descriptions quickly devolved into harmful stereotypes. Africans, Linnaeus claimed, were "crafty" (subtle), "slow" (lazy), "neglectful" (careless), and governed by "judgment" (caprice). Even their physical traits were twisted into caricatures—"flat noses, swollen lips, spreading breasts."

(Skott & Naum, 2019)

These descriptors were not just observations; they were weapons. They reinforced stereotypes that justified colonial exploitation and enslavement. Such narratives were amplified through travel literature of the time, particularly by Dutch colonizers at the Cape of Good Hope, who sought to portray Africans as inherently inferior and incapable of self-governance.

In this description by Linnaeus, Africans were put at the bottom of a hierarchy of human varieties and described as being lazy, cunning, lustful, and careless, among other things. (Hübinette et. al, 2022)

THE LEGACY OF "LESS THAN"

This dehumanization did not remain confined to 18th-century scientific discourse. In the United States, it was enshrined into law. The infamous Three-Fifths Compromise of the Constitution, championed by President James Madison, declared Black people to be only three-fifths of human beings for representation and taxation purposes. This legal codification of inferiority cemented the belief that Black lives were less valuable and less human.

Even in more modern times, these ideologies persist. In 2007, James Watson, a Nobel Prize-winning scientist, infamously remarked to Britain's Sunday Times that he was "gloomy about the prospect of Africa" because he believed African intelligence was genetically lower than that of Europeans. Such remarks, steeped in pseudo-scientific racism, reveal how deeply these colonial lies have permeated even the highest echelons of intellectual thought. (Hübinette et al., 2022)

INTERNALIZING THE LIE

The harm of these ideologies is not limited to external oppression; they have also been internalized by some within the Black community. The narrative of "not being like regular Black folks" reflects an insidious form of self-separation, a coping mechanism born from centuries of stigma. It is the product of a society that has continually equated Blackness with inferiority while holding whiteness as the standard of worth.

Linnaeus's framework categorized humanity into rigid archetypes:

Americanus: Red, choleric (bad-tempered), governed by traditional practices.

Europaeus: White, sanguine (cheerful), governed by religion.

Asiaticus: Sallow, melancholic (sad), governed by opinions.

Africanus: Black, phlegmatic (unemotional), governed by choice.

This hierarchy relegated Africans to the bottom, perpetuating the myth of laziness, cunning, and carelessness. Such ideas have lingered, influencing perceptions and policies that disproportionately disadvantage Black people across the globe.

CHALLENGING THE NARRATIVE

As I reflected on her words, I understood they were not born of malice but of survival. To navigate a world that devalues Blackness, some have adopted narratives that distance themselves from these harmful stereotypes. But true liberation lies in challenging these ideologies—both in society and within us.

Recognizing the historical context of these beliefs is the first step. It allows us to dismantle the colonial frameworks that have shaped them and reclaim the humanity, beauty, and complexity of Black identity. We must replace narratives of inferiority with those of empowerment, pride, and resilience.

For too long, the lie of Black inferiority has cast its shadow over generations. But through education, awareness, and collective action, we can shine a light on the truth: Blackness is not something to escape from but something to embrace.

THE ROOTS OF COLORISM: A STRATEGIC DIVIDE

From the first encounter with colonial powers, the deliberate introduction of colorism was not a happenstance it was a calculated tactic, designed to sow division within Black communities. This strategy not only fractured the unity that might have posed a threat to colonial authority but also established a hierarchy where lighter skin was equated with worth and opportunity. The lighter-skinned individuals, often the offspring of enslaved women and their enslavers, were given privileges access to education, less grueling labor, and sometimes even improved living conditions on the assumption that their proximity to whiteness made them more valuable. But, while they were granted these advantages, they were still subjected to the systemic racism that swept through colonial and societal structures. It is essential to understand that these privileges were never an avenue to freedom. They were merely tools of division, often used to exploit, manipulate, and distance individuals from their true cultural roots.

The tension between lighter-skinned and darker-skinned Black people was not just a matter of individual experience but of communal dissonance. Lighter-skinned people, even with their perceived advantages, faced the harsh reality that racism did not recognize skin tone once their Black identity was confirmed. The infamous "one-drop rule" ensured that regardless of the shade of their skin, they would face discrimination and marginalization for their African ancestry. This left them in a complex and painful position: to some darker-skinned individuals, lighter-skinned people seemed complicit in a system that devalued them, breeding resentment and mistrust. Yet, darker-skinned individuals, bearing the brunt of oppression, were often the ones most deeply affected by the societal devaluation of their complexion, internalizing these biases and perpetuating cycles of marginalization.

PROXIMITY TO WHITENESS AS POWER

For lighter-skinned individuals, their proximity to whiteness often meant a position of power, at least within the confines of colonial structures. They were more likely to secure roles as house servants or intermediaries, tasked with enforcing the oppressive system. This alignment with colonial values, as painful as it was, carried material benefits. However, these benefits, framed within the colonial system, sowed competition within Black communities. It was no longer just about survival; it was about seeking opportunities to assimilate and avoid harsh punishments often by suppressing one's authentic self. As they ascended within this system, however, the ultimate cost was clear: the price of conformity was the erasure of one's cultural identity.

This "colonial costume" was worn by many, an external façade designed to fit Eurocentric ideals of beauty, behaviour, and morality. Yet, what was gained in acceptance from the oppressor often came at the expense of one's inner peace, creating an identity conflict that was both psychological and cultural. Conformity required a betrayal of the self, an abandonment of heritage, and an acceptance of inferiority to an oppressive standard. The price of wearing the colonial costume was not just about external rejection, it was about internalizing the lie that proximity to whiteness would never bring true peace.

THE COLONIAL COSTUME: CONFORMING FOR SURVIVAL

The colonial costume is not a relic of the past, it has echoes in our present day. It continues to influence how people within the Black community navigate societal spaces, often dictating how they present themselves, speak, or even what they value. The historical legacy of colonialism lives on, urging people to conform to Eurocentric standards for the sake of advancement, assimilation, or acceptance. It demands that we erase parts of our identity to fit into a world that refuses to truly embrace who we are. The desire for opportunities or the fear of rejection propels this desire for conformity, yet the cost remains steep. As a community, we are left grappling with the deep psychological wounds of internalized racism and cultural alienation.

The colonial costume is not just a metaphor, it's a lived experience, worn daily by those who believe that success and acceptance lie in distancing themselves from their authentic Blackness. As the world continues to see beauty in Eurocentric features, Black people, both lighter and darker skinned continue to struggle with defining their value. From hair texture to skin tone, we are taught that the closer we come to whiteness, the better our chances for success. But, as we have seen throughout history, this desire for power through assimilation has always been a trap.

COLORISM'S CULTURAL AND SOCIAL IMPACT

The ramifications of colorism extend beyond individual identity. It has shaped African American culture, relationships, and even social dynamics in ways that continue to affect us today. The scars of these systemic divisions are visible in the way we interact with each other, the way we form relationships, and the way we view ourselves.

How often have you heard someone from our community reference a dark-skinned baby or member of their family as their little "chocolate drop"? I've heard this term all too often. I know that it is not out of malice; I believe that this term is applied as a label of love to let the child know that this racially driven society may not value your beautiful black skin, but we do.

The issue with the "chocolate drop" label is that it serves almost as a fore-warning, an announcement, or declaration to society that "this is the dark family member," instead of letting the child grow and know that their black is beautiful. Ironically, we have played into social stratification within our community via colorism. It must be said that regardless of one's intentions, the impact is always greater than the intent. If we continually allow the depth of our family member's complexion to be the focal point and the leading topic of discussion, it will create a negative impact. We must be mindful of this.

Today, colorism affects more than just how we see ourselves. It dictates what is considered beautiful, worthy, and acceptable. Through media and popular culture, Eurocentric beauty standards—fair skin, and straight hair—continue to dominate, leaving little room for the celebration of natural African features. Those who deviate from this ideal may struggle with feelings of inadequacy, while those who fit the mold may feel pressure to maintain a standard that distances them from their roots. This dichotomy fosters an environment where, rather than uniting, we continue to divide ourselves into categories based on proximity to whiteness.

RECLAIMING OUR IDENTITY AND REBUILDING OUR COMMUNITY

So, what is the solution? How do we move beyond the colonial costume and its lingering legacy? It begins with unmasking the deeply ingrained divisions that continue to shape our communities. By recognizing the psychological toll that colorism and internalized racism have taken, we can begin to heal and rebuild our sense of identity. But, as with any historical wound, healing must be collective.

We must begin to challenge not just the external forces of oppression but the internalized systems of colorism that we have allowed to persist within our ranks. This will require us to unlearn centuries of social conditioning that have told us our value lies in how close we are to white ideals. It is about returning to our roots reclaiming the beauty of our Blackness in all its forms and rejecting the idea that we must shrink ourselves to fit into a world that refuses to acknowledge our full humanity.

Healing can't happen in isolation. It requires that we confront the realities of colourism head-on and begin having honest, uncomfortable conversations about its impact. As we work to reclaim our identity, we must also foster solidarity within our community, understanding that healing isn't a solitary journey but one that we must undertake together.

The road to reclaiming our authentic selves and rebuilding a unified Black community is long, but it begins with the recognition of the falsehoods that have divided us. And as we journey towards true liberation, we must remember that in unity lies our strength—and only by shedding the colonial costume can we fully realize the power of our collective identity.

5

THE PRICE OF RESPECTABILITY & THE GOOD HAIR IDEOLOGY

For generations, we've been conditioned to believe that assimilation was the key to acceptance. We were told that if we spoke the "right" way, dressed the "right" way, and acted the "right" way, we could finally be seen as equals. We were taught that distancing ourselves from our roots, our culture, and even our people would grant us access to spaces that were never meant for us in the first place.

But here's the truth: Respectability never saved us. It didn't shield us from racism or dismantle the systems built to exclude us. Instead, it forced us to police ourselves, turning oppression inward and convincing us that the problem wasn't the system, but us.

Nowhere is this more evident than in the conversation around hair, where colonialism and white supremacy still dictate what is considered "acceptable," "professional," and, ultimately, "beautiful."

Texturism; The societal bias against tightly coiled, Afro-textured hair is a direct legacy of colonial oppression. This bias continues to shape the lives of Black people worldwide, extending far beyond mere preference. It is a deeply embedded system of discrimination that elevates looser curls and straighter textures while marginalizing the natural, springy coils that are distinctly African.

The "good hair" ideology was born from this system—weaponized against us, used to divide us, and passed down through generations as a marker of value, status, and beauty. This wasn't by accident; it was by design. Colonial systems deliberately constructed these standards to devalue Black identity and culture, ensuring that we internalized their hierarchy long after their physical rule ended.

This chapter explores the historical roots of textures, their manifestation in our communities today, and how we can begin to dismantle the oppressive standards that were never meant to serve us. True liberation doesn't come from conforming to the colonizer's rules—it comes from unapologetically embracing ourselves, exactly as we are.

THE 70S AND 80S: SHAPED BY MEDIA, DEFINED BY HAIR

Growing up in the late 1970s and early 1980s, TV shows like Good Times and The Jeffersons felt culturally familiar, yet most television programs didn't. They seemed foreign, even though we watched them every day. I suppose that's why they called them "programs."

One program we especially enjoyed was Sunny and Cher. My sister Monique and I would watch it eagerly, we loved the idea of having long, straightened hair parted down the middle, just like Cher's. We would put towels on our heads to mimic her hair, swinging it back and forth in front of the bathroom mirror. As we sang, "You don't have to be a star, baby, to be in my show," we used combs and brushes as microphones, totally caught up in the fantasy.

MA'DEAR'S WIG: A LESSON IN HAIR AND IDENTITY

I spent many weekends at my grandmother Ma'dear's house, along with my sister and cousins. Ma'dear was nothing like her mother, great grandma, Angie Mae. Ma'dear loved all her grandchildren, whether we were light-skinned, dark-skinned, or somewhere in between. She didn't care if we played inside or outside, just as long as we didn't run in and out.

For some reason, I always seemed to break something at her house—though never on purpose! Over time, she came to expect it.

Ma'dear drove a big blue Bonneville car made of pure steel. Its backseat was so wide that six or seven of us could sit across it comfortably. She lived in a duplex on Franklin Street, with a rose bush right out front. The Swaya-Brothers market was just a three-minute walk away. We often spent our afternoons playing jacks on the sidewalk, bouncing a tiny red ball as high as we could and scooping up the metal jacks. Whoever could grab the most jacks in the fastest time won. We also played Chinese jacks, a game with colorful plastic rings that we linked together. Of course, there was always hopscotch and our favorite, two-square with a big plastic bouncy ball that we bought at Swaya-Brothers.

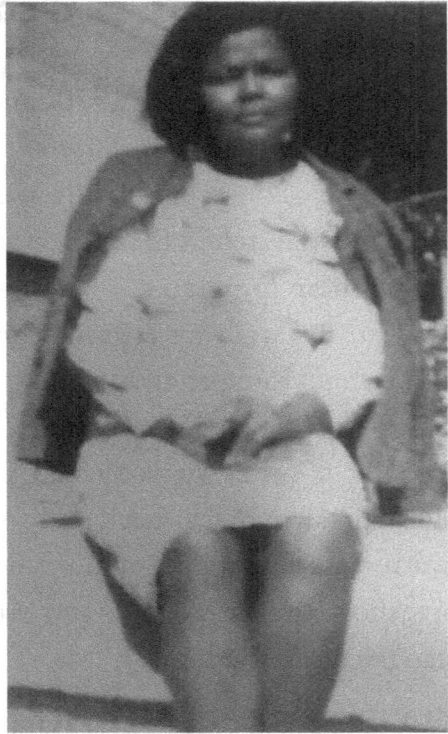

Whenever Ma'dear went to the store, she'd grab us a new ball and some candy—usually a Chic-o-Stick for a nickel. Those were the simple joys of childhood, but what mattered most was the love we felt when we were around her.

One afternoon, while playing two-square out front, the plastic ball popped on Ma'dear's rose bush. She didn't get upset, after all, this had happened all the time. She just walked over to the store and bought another ball.

I, however, was done with the game. I headed inside and noticed something unexpected: two long wigs hanging on Styrofoam doll heads. They looked just like Cher's hair! No more towels on my head, I had the real deal.

I grabbed both wigs and ran outside to show my friend Manuella, who lived next door. She and her family had just arrived, they had just pulled up to their driveway in their station wagon with the side wood panel. I waved the wigs in the air, asking if she wanted to play. She agreed, and soon we were both Cher.

But just as we were pretending to be stars on stage, I saw Ma'dear coming around the corner. What a sight to behold. I knew that I was in trouble. She was fuming. "Gimme my good wig!" she shouted.

As it turned out, Manuella had lice, a fact I had no idea about at the time, as this is not a condition that Black families experience (it's rare, if ever). For Ma'dear, that wig was a priceless possession, and it was ruined. She had to throw it away. Needless to say, Ma'dear sent me to that rose bush to pick a switch. IYKYK!

Straight hair wasn't an obsession for us, but it was certainly portrayed as the "ideal" by the media. In contrast, my mother's perfect afro was everything to me. I would stand next to her as she combed out her hair, dreaming of one day having an afro just like hers. She'd use an afro pick to fluff it out, then toss a beige chiffon scarf into the air, the scarf seemed to slowly billow down in the air, landing perfectly on her hair. She would pat it into

shape, spray it with afro sheen, and remove the scarf—voilà, she was ready.

My mom also had the perfect figure to match her afro, and I longed to be just like her.

The terms "afro" and "natural" were used interchangeably to describe the hairstyle. My dad had a natural too, and they both wore it with pride. During the 70's, embracing our natural hair was part of who we were as Black folk.

THE CURL IS COLONIAL THEFT

By the 1980s, Billie D. Williams was a household name, flaunting his "good hair" on every television screen, and hair texture services were booming. Dr. Willie Morrow, who lived just a few blocks away from us, had invented the California Curl. However, he shared his idea with a man named Jherri Redding, who allegedly stole Dr Morrow's formula, added his twist, and commercialized the curl. Since Redding was already well-connected in Hollywood, the Jheri curl was born, and he took all the credit. *ALLEGEDLY.*

At the time, people were getting "the curl" done in someone's kitchen for just $5 a head, leading to what was called the "kitchen curl."

There was a noticeable shift in how Black people styled their hair. For generations, Black hair had been so versatile, yet we didn't fully understand how to manage it as we do today. I vividly remember the night before Easter when I would stay up late to get my hair done by my sister Monique. She wasn't a professional hairdresser, but like many Black households, we made do with what we had. She'd tell me to shampoo my hair in the shower, then sit me by the stove in the kitchen. It didn't feel quite right, but since she was my older sister, I trusted her. She'd pour baby oil on my wet hair and press it, the sizzling sound accompanying the heat as the oil burned me. Then, she'd roll my hair up in sponge rollers, so I'd be ready for church the next morning. It was a mess but that's probably why I ended up in the beauty industry.

By the mid-80s, my mom had asked her best friend Julie to press my hair. Julie had graduated from Bay Vista Beauty College, and her kitchen was always packed with people waiting for their turn. It felt like a beauty shop there. We couldn't wait for Julie to get her hands in our head. Once she finished with my hair, it had a flow, moving as though I was standing in front of a fan.

Men were just as stylish with their hair. I remember my dad coming home one day, entering through the front door wearing platform shoes and a perm (not a curly perm, but a chemical relaxer) that made his hair resemble James Brown's. My mother nearly passed out when she saw him. "What in the world did you do to your hair?" she asked. He looked like a 1970s superfly pimp. I loved how his hair moved, not so much for him but for me. I wanted my hair to look like that, so I begged my mom to get me a relaxer. She took me to Willie Morrow's salon on Market Street. He had just created a new relaxer called the Ocean Wave Relaxer, and I came out of there like a new person. I loved it!

Little did we know that colonialism had impacted on how we saw ourselves, especially our hair. Our self-perception had been colonized. The beauty standards we adopted were Eurocentric, and this included how we viewed our natural curls and textures. But let's explore how all this came to be.

Hair texturism is rooted in racism, a form of discrimination that can be traced back to nineteenth and early twentieth-century physical anthropology. At that time, hair was thought to be a key marker of racial distinctions (Tarlo, 2019). In the 1900s, German professor and eugenicist Eugen Fischer created a hair gauge to assess the "whiteness" of mixed-race individuals in what is now Namibia. The pencil test, used in apartheid-era South Africa, helped determine a person's racial identity based on how easily a pencil could be inserted into their hair. If the pencil slid out, the person was considered "coloured" (mixed-race); if the pencil stayed in, they were considered Black.

Oprah Winfrey's hair stylist, Andre Walker, re-introduced the idea of a hair typing system. Label hair from straight to tightly coiled with a numbering system that identifies straight hair as 1a to tightly coiled at 4c. As a hair stylist and professor of cosmetology, I do not like the curl pattern numbering system. I prefer to identify the hair by its texture and curl pattern; no one will fit perfectly in one category. On the flip side, many clients find that having a system to determine their curl pattern is good for them.

Once again, this is another way of categorizing, and sadly, people are placing a stigma and/or a negative connotation on having 4c (tightly coiled) hair, which ironically finds itself at the bottom of this labeling system.

WOMEN HAIRCARE PIONEERS

The story of Black haircare innovation is one of resilience, creativity, and an enduring legacy of empowerment. At the forefront of this transformative journey were two extraordinary women: Sarah Breedlove, famously known as Madame C.J. Walker, and Annie Minerva Turnbo Malone. Both women not only revolutionized haircare but also redefined beauty and femininity for African American women in the 20th century.

Madame C.J. Walker is often celebrated as the first Black woman millionaire, credited with creating haircare products specifically for Black women. Her contributions were groundbreaking, yet history reveals that Annie Malone, a lesser known but equally remarkable figure, may have claimed this milestone first. Annie Malone was more than just a businesswoman; she was a visionary. As the creator and president of Poro College—the first Black-owned cosmetology school in the United States, established in 1918 in St. Louis, Missouri—Malone played a pivotal role in shaping the Black beauty industry. Her influence extended beyond education, as Poro College expanded to open 32 more beauty schools across the United States.

Although Malone's legacy has often been overshadowed by the fame of her former student and business rival, Madame C.J. Walker, their collective contributions remain undeniable. As Reese (2013) notes, both women were instrumental in redefining beauty and empowering African American women during a time when societal norms sought to marginalize them. Through their pioneering efforts, they built a foundation for generations of innovation in Black beauty culture.

Black women have always been trailblazers in the beauty industry. From the early 20th century to today, this spirit of innovation continues to thrive. Annie Malone and Madame C.J. Walker not only addressed the unique haircare needs of Black women but also created spaces for empowerment, self-expression, and financial independence. Their impact reverberates far beyond the products they created—it's in the confidence they inspired and the opportunities they unlocked for countless women.

Their influence reminds me of my friend and beauty industry innovator, Ms. Tammy Golden. Following in the footsteps of Malone and Walker, Tammy embodies the same spirit of resilience and creativity that has defined Black beauty culture for over a century. Her groundbreaking product line, The Silk Out System, represents the next chapter of innovation in haircare. Just as Malone and Walker revolutionized beauty in their time, Tammy is making her mark today, ensuring that the legacy of excellence in Black haircare continues to thrive.

The stories of Annie Malone and Madame C.J. Walker are not just tales of business success, they are testaments to the power of vision, determination, and community. They remind us that beauty is more than skin deep; it is a form of self-affirmation and resistance. These women redefined what it meant to be beautiful and created spaces where African American women could embrace their identities unapologetically.

As we celebrate their contributions, we also honor the contemporary pioneers who continue their work. Annie Malone and Madame C.J. Walker would undoubtedly be proud of today's innovators, like Tammy Golden, who carry forward their legacy with creativity and passion.

TEXTURE TALK

The roots of texturism are colonial, born from racist ideals that associated looser hair textures with humanity, beauty, and worth. Those with straighter hair were often given less labor-intensive tasks, reinforcing the perception that such hair was more desirable. Over time, this belief became ingrained, leading to the "good hair" narrative that persists. This narrative has caused pain and division, particularly within families, as biases against tightly coiled hair can create feelings of inferiority or pressure to conform.

The impact of texturism stretches beyond self-image. In the professional world, natural hair is often scrutinized, with styles like afros, braids, and locs deemed unprofessional. Media representations of beauty reinforce these Eurocentric standards, marginalizing natural Black hair. But resistance is growing. The "Black is Beautiful" campaign of the 1960s and the CROWN Act of 2019 are key milestones in challenging these stereotypes. The "Black is Beautiful" campaign, which emerged during the Civil Rights Movement, rejected Eurocentric beauty ideals and championed natural Black features. Figures like Nina Simone and Kathleen Cleaver became symbols of this transformation.

Building on their efforts, the CROWN Act was introduced in 2019 to address discrimination against natural hair in workplaces and schools. The Act protects individuals who wear natural hairstyles like braids, twists, afros and locs from being discriminated against based on their appearance. This legislation has made a significant impact, marking a step toward inclusivity for Black individuals in all areas of society.

Social media has further amplified these efforts, creating platforms where Black individuals can share their experiences and celebrate the beauty of their natural hair. These movements represent more than just aesthetics, they are a reclamation of culture, identity, and self-worth.

UNDERSTANDING TEXTURISM

Texturism is the preferential treatment of certain hair textures, typically straighter or looser curls—over tightly coiled or kinky hair. Its origins lie in colonial ideals that equate proximity to whiteness with beauty and worth. During slavery, lighter-skinned individuals with straighter hair were seen as closer to Eurocentric standards of beauty and were treated preferentially. This bias became ingrained in societal norms and passed down from generation to generation.

The preference for "manageable" or "silky" hair became a symbol of social status and acceptance. Over time, this preference for straightened or relaxed hair became embedded in communities, industries, and families, dictating many people's choices and reinforcing harmful beauty standards. Today, the cycle continues as many Black people still rely on relaxers, straighteners, or wigs to conform to a Eurocentric idea of beauty.

THE "GOOD HAIR" NARRATIVE

The concept of "good hair" has long reflected and reinforced Eurocentric beauty standards. It refers to hair that is straighter, wavier, or loosely curled, while tightly coiled hair is often deemed "bad" or undesirable. This narrative, born out of systemic oppression, perpetuated harmful beauty ideals that continue to affect society today.

Historically, "good hair" was seen as a ticket to social and economic mobility. Lighter-skinned individuals with straighter hair were more likely to be hired or promoted in professional settings, reinforcing the idea that certain hair textures were more acceptable. This notion extended into personal relationships, where some individuals and families preferred that their children or romantic partners have "good hair". For those whose hair didn't fit this standard, feelings of shame and alienation became common.

NYABINGHI HAIR

Tightly coiled hair, often misunderstood and unfairly pathologized, is nothing short of divine artistry. It defies gravity, reaching toward the sun as if echoing the resilience and beauty of the people who bear it. It's time to reframe the narrative. Tightly coiled hair is not "nappy" but blessed an affirmation of individuality and cultural pride. As the saying goes, "Who God has blessed, no man can curse."

This was a lesson my nephew Derick, affectionately called Tikki, learned one transformative day at the World-Famous Imperial Barber Shop in San Diego. While I often cut his hair myself, on particularly busy weeks, I entrusted him to Mr Tau, a barber whose reputation for combining cultural awareness with community care made his shop a sanctuary for Black boys and men alike.

Barber shops like Mr. Tau's are more than places to get a haircut, they're spaces where history, identity, and culture intersect. As soon as we stepped inside, Mr Tau welcomed Tikki with a firm handshake, a piercing yet kind gaze, and the powerful words: "Welcome, young man." This moment was more than a simple greeting; it was a rite of passage, a reminder that he was stepping into a community of strong, conscious Black men who value their heritage.

The scene brought back memories of my time in the 1990s at ISIS Beauty and Barber Salon, where Brotha Carl, a devout Muslim and upstanding family man, nurtured the Black community with love and intention. Mr. Tau's barber shop mirrored that ethos. It wasn't just about grooming hair;

it was about grooming confidence, pride, and connection to one's roots.

As Tikki sat in the chair, his tightly coiled hair springing like rubber bands, his eyes widened when Mr. Tau took out an afro pick. Sensing his apprehension, Mr. Tau smiled and said,

"Naw, man, you've got that good Nyabinghi hair."

The word sparked curiosity:

"Nyabinghi?" Tikki asked. Mr Tau explained,

"Yes, Nyabinghi. It's powerful, rhythmic, and connected to our roots."

The term "Nyabinghi" carries profound cultural weight. Originating from East Africa as a symbol of resistance, it was later adopted by Jamaican Rastafari in the 20th century. Nyabinghi gatherings, marked by chanting, drumming, and singing, celebrate unity, spiritual resistance, and liberation. Bob Marley's "Jump Nyabinghi" introduced many to this tradition, though its depth often went unrecognized by broader audiences. As Richard (2024) notes, Nyabinghi is both a spiritual practice and a form of cultural resistance, celebrating freedom and Black power.

Wow, so Nyabinghi hair is beautiful, natty... rhythmic, culturally dancing to the beat of the African djimbe drum, ready to dread!

That day, as Tikki left the barber shop with a fresh cut and newfound pride, he looked in the mirror, gave himself the old once over, and declared with a grin,

"Yeah... I've got that good Nyabinghi hair!"

His words were a triumph, a sign that he had embraced his identity with confidence and joy.

THE "GOOD HAIR" NARRATIVE IN CONTEMPORARY SOCIETY

The "good hair" narrative persists in modern society, though often in subtler forms. Hair product advertisements still promote "taming" or "smoothing" unruly hair, perpetuating the belief that natural curls need correction. Media representations continue to favour straight or loosely curled hair, limiting the visibility of more diverse Black hair textures. These portrayals influence self-image, particularly for young Black children, who may internalize the idea that their natural hair is less beautiful or acceptable.

The media and beauty industries have historically played significant roles in perpetuating texturism. For years, hair product ads emphasized the need to "relax" or "straighten" natural hair for a polished or professional look. These campaigns suggested that straight hair was linked to success, while natural textures were often seen as incompatible with upward mobility.

Entertainment also reinforced these ideals. Characters with Eurocentric hairstyles were often cast as protagonists or romantic leads, while those with natural textures were relegated to secondary or stereotypical roles. This lack of representation has shaped societal attitudes, pressuring individuals to conform to texturist standards.

However, in recent years, there has been a shift toward better representation of natural hair in media and advertising. Celebrities, influencers, and campaigns now celebrate diverse Black hair textures, challenging the dominance of Eurocentric beauty norms. Despite these strides, the legacy of texturism remains, requiring continued efforts to dismantle these entrenched biases.

The natural hair movement represents a powerful form of resistance against textures. By embracing their natural textures, individuals reclaim their self-worth and celebrate their Black identity. For many, the transition from chemically altered hair to natural textures is a deeply personal journey, one that requires overcoming internalized biases and societal judgment.

Social media has played a crucial role in amplifying these efforts, providing platforms for Black creators to share hair care tips, celebrate natural styles, and build supportive communities. These spaces have become hubs of empowerment, challenging decades of texture norms and creating visibility for diverse hair textures.

THE ROLE OF TEXTURISM IN SHAPING IDENTITY

Texturism doesn't just affect personal experiences, it has broader cultural and societal implications. In professional settings, Black individuals with natural hair often face discrimination, whether through overt bias or microaggressions about "professionalism." While natural hair is becoming more accepted, the beauty industry still profits from products and services that alter natural textures, showing that the influence of colonial beauty standards persists.

Nevertheless, the resistance against texturism reflects the strength and resilience of the Black community. By rejecting the "good hair" myth, individuals and communities are challenging systemic biases and redefining beauty standards. This ongoing effort celebrates the diversity of Black identity, asserting that natural hair is a powerful and beautiful part of who we are.

DISMANTLING TEXTURISM

For generations, Black people have been told that their beauty, especially their hair, wasn't good enough. But the truth is, we were never the problem. Dismantling texturism is not only about rejecting the "good hair" myth but also about rejecting all colonial remnants that tell us we are not enough. It's about dismantling the false hierarchies that have divided us for centuries and reimagining beauty on our terms.

This fight goes beyond individual hair care. It's about collective movement, ensuring that the next generation of Black children grows up free from toxic beauty standards. It's about creating spaces where natural hair is accepted without question and dismantling systems that still police our hair in schools, workplaces, and media.

The journey toward self-acceptance and collective empowerment begins with embracing the beauty inherent in natural hair. By celebrating the full spectrum of Black hair textures, we move closer to a future where authenticity is not just accepted—it is celebrated.

To love yourself fully means loving all of you, including your hair.

6

PROXIMITY TO WHITENESS AND SOCIAL STRATIFICATION

We were taught that if we got closer, closer to whiteness, closer to their beauty standards, closer to their way of speaking, dressing, and thinking then maybe, just maybe, we'd be safe. We were sold the lie that if we distanced ourselves from our Blackness, we could carve out space in a world that was never built for us.

But proximity to whiteness has never been a shield, only a leash. It was designed to control, divide, and keep us forever chasing an approval that will never come. The psychological conditioning born from colonial rule planted the seeds of this deception, ensuring that generations of Black people internalized the false belief that aligning with Eurocentric ideals would grant them power, upward mobility, and security.

This was never about progress; it was about control. The illusion of acceptance was nothing more than a tool to fracture our unity, making us see each other as competitors rather than kin. And the cost of buying into this illusion? Generations of internalized racism, self-rejection, and community division.

In this chapter, I will peel back the layers of this deception examining how colonialism manipulated our self-perception, how proximity to whiteness became a false currency, and how we can begin the process of rejecting these lies and reclaiming our full, unapologetically Blackness.

THE FLIGHT ATTENDANT

This desire for proximity to whiteness comes with a cost. I remember boarding a short flight from San Diego to Las Vegas; I was taking my dad and a close family friend, DD, for a fun-filled weekend getaway. We met an older Black woman in the airport, who would be seated two aisles behind us. We were in the very first row near the cockpit, having boarded the plane first.

As I sat down, I heard,

"Aht aht... put that up."

A Black male flight attendant was pointing at my waist. I was wearing a fanny pack, and he said,

"That's gotta go up there."

Gesturing to the overhead compartment. I was caught off guard by his matter-of-fact tone. No worries, I immediately took the fanny pack off and stored it in the overhead compartment. As I did so, I told him,

"I always fly with it on and never had any issues, but no worries, I already put it up."

He swiftly approached me, turned sharply, wagging his finger side to side, and scornfully said,

"One thing you don't do is tell a flight attendant what you did on a previous flight."

He quickly turned away, grabbing the intercom device to announce to the passengers boarding. I couldn't believe what I was experiencing.

Then, he began to yell over the intercom,

"Turn that thing off or use your headset."

I looked around, trying to identify who he was talking to, when I realized it was the older Black woman seated two rows behind us. She had been talking into her watch/phone-type gadget. I told him that he shouldn't speak to her that way. He rolled his eyes in disdain for her and me, then continued preparing for takeoff.

As he buckled into the jump seat next to his redhead colleague, he leaned in and whispered,

"It's always US; that is a problem."

As he said, "US," he rubbed his wrist with his index finger, signaling that by "US," he meant Black people. I shook my head at the depth of internalized racism within him. How could he, a Black man, perpetuate this harmful stereotype to his white colleague?

I asked him, "Excuse me, when you said 'us,' were you referring to Black people?" With a quick snap of his neck and a long eye roll, he replied,

"If I were talking about Black people, I would have said so!"

"No, you wouldn't have,"

I responded, realizing this wasn't about me or the older woman, it was about his internal conflict. He thought he was gaining proximity to whiteness at our expense. The sad part? He didn't even realize that he, too, was suffering. Beneath that uniform, I could see that he wore his colonial costume, and it came with a cape.

This moment exemplifies how internalized racism and colonialism shape behavior and self-perception. His actions reflected a mindset that distances himself from Blackness, reinforcing harmful divisions within our community. His belief that aligning with whiteness grants him more value only perpetuates the cycle of self-rejection and division.

THE ROLE OF MEDIA AND EDUCATION IN PROMOTING EUROCENTRIC VALUES

Colonial systems strategically used media and education to elevate whiteness as the ultimate standard of beauty, intelligence, and worth. Textbooks glorified European history while erasing or marginalizing African contributions, leaving generations of African Americans disconnected from their heritage and unaware of their ancestors' profound impact on the development of the United States. Media reinforced this narrative by idolizing European features as the epitome of success and desirability. This created a psychological burden, fostering a cycle of internalized inferiority that continues to affect the African American community today.

These damaging messages didn't just shape external perceptions—they infiltrated personal and communal identities, influencing family dynamics and self-perception. Children absorbed these ideals through stories, lessons, and media. This erosion of cultural pride became entrenched in a system designed to erase and invalidate Black identity.

The 1968 documentary Black History: Lost, Stolen or Strayed, narrated by Bill Cosby, powerfully illustrates the consequences of these distorted narratives. The film highlights how the achievements and contributions of Americans of African descent were systematically excluded from American history education while pervasive derogatory stereotypes diminished Black identity and culture.

CLARK DOLL EXPERIMENT

One poignant moment in the documentary re-creates the 1958 Clark doll experiment, or the "doll test," where Black children overwhelmingly chose white dolls over Black dolls as prettier, smarter, or better. This stark example reveals the deep-rooted impact of internalized racism, shaped by a media landscape that equated beauty and worth with whiteness while devaluing Blackness. Mamie and Kenneth Clark (Clark and Clark, 1958) first highlighted how Black children, in the "Doll Study" experiment, overwhelmingly selected the white doll as nice and the Black doll as looking bad and mean (Parsons et al., 2019).

The irony here is not lost: it is common, even today, for Black parents to purchase white dolls for their children. Yet, white parents rarely, if ever purchase Black dolls for their children.

Black people, ask yourself; as a child, did your parents ever purchase a white doll for you to play with, or did any of your Black friends have white dolls to play with?

I am willing to bet that there is a strong possibility that you answered "yes", you did have at least one white doll, if not all white dolls to play with as a child.

If your parents intentionally bought you Black dolls, I applaud them, as they understood the importance of representation.

Now, for non-Black people, ask yourself; as a child, did your parents ever purchase a Black doll for you to play with, or did any of your non-Black friends have Black dolls to play with?

I am willing to bet that there is a strong possibility that you answered "no", that you never had at least one Black doll as a child.

For the non-Black people who answered "no," this points to a larger framework of symbolic interactionism. I'm not saying that white families should rush out and buy Black dolls for their children, but it would be a teachable moment to expose children to diversity in their toys, and no, this does not make for bad parents who do not. This was just my observation.

My point is that the Black community has been socialized to default to whiteness without a second thought. How many white Barbies have appeared under the Christmas trees of Black households? Ironically, as I write this text, it is Christmas morning. I can't help but wonder how many white dolls are under the tree awaiting to be unwrapped by a happy little Black girl.

No, I'm not exempt. As a child, I, too, had white dolls. But now, I realize that representation matters. Black folks, be intentional about buying your child a doll that looks like them. And to the parents who already do this, I commend you. When children only see beauty in someone who doesn't look like them, it's hard for them to see beauty within themselves. This subtle yet powerfully damaging psychological impact has been perpetuated for generations.

The long-term effects of these narratives extend beyond individual self-perception to community dynamics, influencing how Black people view themselves and one another. By revisiting works like Black History: Lost, Stolen, or Strayed, we are reminded of the urgent need to dismantle these harmful ideals and reclaim the richness and diversity of African American history and culture. Reclaiming this narrative is not just about correcting the past, but about fostering pride, unity, and authenticity within the Black community. Reclaiming our history means rejecting colonial lies and embracing the beauty of our Blackness.

THE PURSUIT OF SOCIAL STRATIFICATION AND ITS CONSEQUENCES

The narrative that proximity to whiteness could alter societal perceptions has been a deeply problematic force within the African diaspora. In a world shaped by systemic racism, this pursuit of social stratification, climbing the societal ladder through assimilation, was often seen as a survival mechanism. Adopting Eurocentric aesthetics, speech patterns, and behaviours became a way to navigate an oppressive society and access opportunities otherwise denied. However, this approach carried profound consequences.

For many, the constant effort to conform created a painful tension between societal expectations and authentic cultural identity. The psychological toll of living in this duality led to feelings of shame, disconnection, and an enduring sense of being an outsider in both spaces.

This phenomenon is captured by the term "house knee-grow" mentality, referring to the divisions created during slavery. As discussed earlier, lighter-skinned individuals or those perceived as closer to whiteness were often granted privileges. Though these privileges weren't freedom, they reinforced the idea that proximity to whiteness offered a path to survival and advancement in a system that perpetuated such divisions.

The "house knee-grow" mentality also fostered a culture of compliance with oppressive systems. Those who benefited from their perceived proximity to whiteness may have internalized a sense of superiority, consciously or unconsciously aligning their values with the dominant culture. This often led to alienation from their community, as they were seen as complicit in reinforcing oppressive structures. Meanwhile, darker-skinned individuals bore the brunt of overt discrimination while grappling with internalized racism that devalued their features and identities.

The result was a fractured community, weakened by divisions that hampered solidarity and resistance, fulfilling the colonial agenda of control through fragmentation. This legacy lingers today, influencing perceptions of beauty, intelligence, and worth within the Black community. Recognizing and addressing the "house knee-grow" mentality is key to dismantling these divisions and fostering unity.

PSYCHOLOGICAL TOLL: IMPOSTER SYNDROME AND ISOLATION

The psychological toll of striving for proximity to whiteness cannot be overstated. For those seeking acceptance through assimilation, feelings of imposter syndrome were common. Despite conforming to societal norms, many still felt like perpetual outsiders, never truly accepted by the dominant culture, and increasingly disconnected from their community. This tension led to alienation, shame, and a fragmented sense of identity.

The "every man for himself" mentality, a product of systemic oppression, deepened divisions within the African American community. This mindset emerged as a survival mechanism in a world where opportunities were scarce, and competition for essential resources was fierce. Faced with the relentless pressures of systemic racism, many individuals prioritized their advancement, often at the expense of collective solidarity.

This shift eroded the mutual support networks that once sustained resilience within the community. Families, neighbourhoods, and organizations that had thrived on unity began to fragment as individuals focused inward, navigating a system that rewarded compliance and assimilation over collaboration.

This strain on relationships created a ripple effect that weakened the community's ability to mobilize against systemic injustice. The prioritization of self-preservation fostered mistrust, competition, and resentment, further isolating individuals. This division played directly into the hands of oppressive systems that relied on fragmentation to maintain control. Without collective strength, efforts for systemic change were often stymied or diluted. The "every man for himself" mentality disrupted the sense of interconnectedness that once provided strength and perpetuated the very inequality it sought to escape.

Recognizing and addressing this mindset is critical for rebuilding trust, solidarity, and the resilience needed to create lasting change.

THE TIME FOR CHANGE IS NOW: A REVOLUTION LONG OVERDUE

We have confronted the lies. We have unpacked the trauma. We have reclaimed our identities. Now, the question is no longer "What's wrong?"—we've answered that enough. The real question is, "What are we going to do about it?"

Understanding oppression is not enough. Awareness without action is useless. It is time long past time to dismantle the systems that have kept us bound, stop waiting for change and start creating it.

But what does real change look like? What does revolution mean in the 21st century?

We don't need to start from scratch, we've been here before. The Civil Rights Movement laid the foundation, but it wasn't just about marching, sit-ins, and speeches. It was about economic empowerment, legal battles, and policy reform. The Black Panthers understood this when they built programs that fed children, educated people, and provided healthcare which the government refused. That was self-determination. That was a revolution.

Now, we take what worked and bring it into today's world, with the tools and technology of our time.

Black-Owned Infrastructure: We must reclaim ownership—of our businesses, schools, and media. Instead of waiting for a seat at someone else's table, we build our own. Support Black banks. Invest in Black startups. Develop co-ops and mutual aid networks that sustain our economic power.

Tech-Driven Education: The knowledge gap is a tool of oppression. We must control our education—not just within schools but beyond them. Black-led online platforms, digital libraries, coding programs, and mentorship networks should teach financial literacy, STEM, and entrepreneurship to our youth.

Community Health & Wellness: Healthcare in America was never built for us—so we create our own. Like the Black Panthers provided free clinics, we expand that vision with Black-led wellness centres, mental health initiatives, and holistic healing spaces. Virtual therapy, telehealth, and mobile clinics must serve our communities on our terms.

Food Security & Sustainability: We must nourish our people—literally. Community gardens, urban farming, and Black-owned grocery co-ops ensure our neighbourhoods are no longer food deserts. With technology, we can implement smart agriculture, hydroponics, and localized food production to feed our people without relying on external systems.

Political and Social Power: Protesting is not enough. We must infiltrate policy, draft legislation, and control local economies. We need a modern Freedom School movement, educating ourselves on policy, law, and governance so that we're not just demanding justice; we are writing the laws that define it.

This is what the next revolution looks like, not asking, not waiting, but building, strategizing, and reclaiming.

The future of our people does not depend on how well we assimilate, but how boldly we stand in our power. True freedom has never been about proximity to whiteness—it's about our ability to define, sustain, and uplift ourselves.

We are not waiting for change. We are the change.

7

HEALING THE WOUNDS

The fight for Black liberation is not just about a single moment, it's a continuous, evolving movement. Every generation before us has fought their battle, and now, it is our turn. The choices we make today, what we teach our children, how we challenge oppression, and how we build community, will determine whether we break the cycle or allow it to continue.

We are standing at a crossroads. The lessons of history are clear: the system was never meant to serve us. We've spent centuries waiting for justice, for fairness, for a seat at a table that was never built with us in mind. But why should we keep waiting? Why should we keep asking for permission to exist freely?

Our ancestors didn't wait. They created. They fought. They built. They knew that true power does not come from begging for acceptance but from reclaiming what was stolen and forging our path.

This chapter is about the future. It is about what we leave behind for the next generation. The revolution does not belong to the past, it belongs to us right now.

It is no longer enough to talk about healing. The time for action is overdue. We must move beyond awareness and into transformation. We must build new systems that center on Black identity, empowerment, and self-sufficiency. We must ask: What does real change look like?

Before healing can begin, we must confront the reality of our shared history. The scars left by internalized racism and systemic oppression manifest in fractured relationships, diminished self-worth, and community divisions. These wounds were intentionally inflicted to sow mistrust and erode solidarity. Recognizing this truth is essential because it allows us to view these struggles not as personal failings but as the enduring effects of deliberate strategies.

Healing, however, is not linear. It is a layered and multifaceted process that demands patience, introspection, and collective action. It calls for unlearning the biases that have shaped our perceptions and behaviors while reclaiming pride in our cultural identity. This work is deeply personal, yet its impact radiates outward to strengthen families, communities, and future generations.

Music has always been a powerful tool for resistance and healing, and reggae is a testament to this truth. Born from the African diaspora, reggae channels the pain of oppression into a force for unity, empowerment, and justice. Artists like

Bob Marley, Peter Tosh, Eek-a-Mouse, and my favourite, Steel Pulse, have used their music to challenge systems of inequality, inspire resilience, and call for collective action.

In 1963, Haile Selassie I, emperor of Ethiopia (a country that was never colonized), gave a poignant speech to the United Nations General Assembly, saying:

"Until the philosophy which holds one race superior, and another inferior is finally and permanently discredited and abandoned, everywhere is war. And until there are no longer first-class and second-class citizens of any nation until the color of a man's skin is of no more significance than the color of his eyes, and until basic human rights are equally guaranteed to all without regard to race, there is war. And until that day, the dream of lasting peace, world citizenship, and rule of international morality will remain but a fleeting illusion to be pursued but never attained... now everywhere is war".

- Haile Selassie I

If those words sound familiar, they should. Bob Marley quoted Haile Selassie I's speech, word for word, in his powerful song, "War."

Consider Bob Marley's "Redemption Song" with its passionate plea: "Emancipate yourselves from mental slavery; none but ourselves can free our minds." This lyric encapsulates the essence of healing, by reminding us that we must decolonize our minds and break free from the internalized narratives that devalue our worth.

David Hinds, the innovative lead singer of the world-renowned reggae band Steel Pulse, reminds us to "rock against racism and to rock against fascism and that we are all

Ethiopians (we just don't know it yet)." One of my absolute favourite Steel Pulse songs, "Rally Round the Flag," is a rallying cry that resonates deeply within me, urging communities to stand together against oppression. The powerful song lyrics tell us that:

"Our history is no more a mystery"

"I curse that day...the day they made us slaves."

This song speaks to the testament of Jamaican political activist Marcus Garvey, who, in 1920, created the Pan-African flag to serve as a unifying symbol to connect people of African descent across the globe. "Rally Round the Flag" identifies the meanings of the colours of the flag, stating that:

"Marcus said red is for the blood that flows like the river, Marcus said green is for the land Africa, Marcus said...yellow is for the gold that THEY stole, Marcus said...Black is for the people they looted from."

These lyrics are powerful; I could replay this song repeatedly; in fact, I do—it's my ringtone.

Similarly, Peter Tosh's "Equal Rights" demands justice and reminds us that unity is essential in the fight for equality. Peter Tosh, a core member of the Wailers band (Bob Marley and the Wailers), is said to have taught Marley to play the guitar.

Whenever I visit Jamaica, our family friend "Sexy Rexy," Rexy Thomlison, an outgoing native of Westmorland, Jamaica, declares that "Black is Beautiful." When I visit the island, Rexy takes me to Peter Tosh's home to see Tosh's cousin, Donovan (Neville Powell). Donovan told me that Peter Tosh loved to walk barefoot on their land, and ground himself to the earth, and I removed my shoes and did the same thing when I was there. Peter Tosh would pick fresh lemon grass with other herbs and make healing tea for the body. As descendants from the African continent, we must resort to our ancestors' natural healing practices.

Eek-a-Mouse's song, "Remember," asks whether we remember those days of slavery. While we, in this generation, did not experience slavery firsthand, epigenetics prove that our bodies recognize it. This memory is locked in our DNA, allowing for a change in how our genes are expressed. Our bodies remember; the memories have been downloaded like a computer file. It is not on us; it is in us, and we must never forget!

These songs are not just entertainment; they are blueprints for transformation. They provide space for reflection and a reminder of our shared resilience. As we listen, we reconnect with our identity and draw strength from the wisdom of the past. All the while, the drumbeat stirs something within our core. This is the sound of healing. As we are all on a frequency, the question becomes: What frequency are we vibrating?

STEPS TOWARD HEALING

Healing is not just an individual journey—it is a collective awakening. To truly break free from the psychological chains of oppression, we must turn inward and confront the ways internalized racism has shaped our self-perception. But reflection alone is not enough. We must actively reclaim what was stripped from us— our pride, our culture, our unity. Music, literature, and art have always been tools of resistance, carrying the stories of our ancestors and the truths we were never meant to embrace. It's time to listen, to learn, and to reconnect with the essence of who we are. And we start by:

1. **Personal Reflection and Growth**: Healing begins within. The first step is reflecting on how internalized racism has shaped our beliefs and behaviors. Journaling, meditation, and open conversations about these struggles can help us unearth and challenge harmful narratives. Reggae music offers a lens for introspection—listen deeply and ask: What emotions does this song evoke? How does its message resonate with my journey?

2. **Reclaiming Cultural Pride**: Reconnecting with our history, art, and traditions is a powerful way to reclaim identity. Dive into literature by Black authors, support artists who celebrate African American culture, and participate in events that honor our heritage. By immersing ourselves in these expressions, we reaffirm the beauty and strength of our shared experiences.

3. **Building Unity Within the Community**: Healing cannot happen in isolation. Host community dialogues inspired by themes in reggae and other cultural movements. These conversations can serve as bridges, fostering understanding and collaboration. Through shared stories and mutual support, we rebuild trust and lay the groundwork for collective progress.

While healing addresses the pain of the past, envisioning the future redefines our path forward. We must reimagine beauty, success, and worth based on our values and diversity, not the imposed standards. Let us celebrate the rich spectrum of Black identity, from the variety of skin tones to the natural textures of our hair.

Pursuing unity requires replacing the divisive "every man for himself" mentality with a spirit of solidarity. By supporting Black-owned businesses, mentoring the next generation, and advocating for policies that uplift the community, we create a foundation for lasting change. The future we envision is one where the next generation will grow free from the burdens of internalized oppression, empowered to thrive in a society that values their contributions and identity.

A CALL TO ACTION

Real change is not just a dream, it is a blueprint waiting to be activated. The Civil Rights Movement gave us the roadmap, and the Black Panthers laid the foundation. Now, it's time for a 21st-century revolution that reflects the needs of our people today.

We must rebuild what was lost, our schools, our economic systems, and our media. We must reclaim our power the way our ancestors intended: through education, unity, and self-determination.

The Panthers understood that knowledge was liberation. They created free schools, and literacy programs, and taught Black history unapologetically. Today, we have digital platforms, social media, and community-driven schools that can empower us to take back control of our narratives. We don't need approval to educate our children; we need commitment.

The Panthers didn't just talk about oppression; they addressed it where it hurt the most—in our access to food, healthcare, and well-being. Their Free Breakfast Program fed thousands of Black children daily, proving that when we take care of our own, we thrive. Today, we must demand Black-owned grocery stores, urban farming initiatives, and mental health services rooted in our experiences.

In the age of technology, we have more tools at our disposal than ever before. We must reclaim our economic power by supporting Black-owned businesses, creating cooperative networks, and ensuring our dollars circulate within our communities. Financial literacy, cryptocurrency, and entrepreneurship are not just pathways to wealth; they are pathways to liberation.

We no longer need validation from mainstream platforms. We must create and control our media, networks, streaming services, and content that tells our stories authentically. No more diluted versions of our history. No more narratives that erase our struggle. Our voices must be heard, loud and clear.

This is what liberation looks like.

Let's be clear: It's repatriation time! However our psyche and mental healing is left for us to heal, no one can do that for us. No government, no institution, no outside force. This is our responsibility. Our power. Our revolution.

FINAL WORDS: THE ANTHEM OF LIBERATION

As this chapter closes, we are reminded of the power within our grasp. Healing and unity are not abstract concepts but achievable realities when approached with intention and courage. We must live with purpose, on purpose.

We take our lessons from the music, from the movements, and from the ancestors who paved the way.

Steel Pulse's Rally Round the Flag is our anthem:

Marcus said.

"Red is for the blood that flows like a river. Green is for the land, Africa. Yellow is for the gold that THEY stole. And black is for the people they looted from".

Bob Marley sings:

"Oh, pirates yes they rob I, sold I to the merchant ships" …

"Didn't my people before me, slave for this country…

These are not just lyrics; they are instructions. We must reclaim our narrative. We must build a legacy of pride and power. We must ensure that our children never have to question their worth, their history, or their place in this world.

The work to our collective healing doesn't stop.

Although we've been dealt an eternal black eye, we did not go blind, and if God has given us the vision, indeed, He will provide the provision! Our solution begins with our revolution! Our healing starts now!

-Tosh

Suggested Reggae Songs
(Reggae songs that speak to our plight)

By Bob Marley: War, Redemption Song, Crazy
Baldheads, Keep on Moving

By Peter Tosh: Equal Rights, African

By Eek-a-Mouse: Do You Remember?

By Junior Byles: Fade Away

By Steel Pulse: Wild Goose Chase, Don't Shoot

My all-time favorite by Steel Pulse: Rally Round the
Flag

REFERENCES

Alvarez, A. J., & Farinde-Wu, A. (2022). Advancing a Holistic Trauma Framework for Collective Healing from Colonial Abuses. AERA Open, 8(1).

Degruy, J. (2005). Post traumatic slave syndrome: America's legacy of enduring injury and healing: Degruy, joy A: 9780985217273: Amazon.com: Books. https://www.amazon.com/Post-Traumatic-Slave-Syndrome-Americas/dp/0985217278

James, D., & Iyer, K. (2024). Internalized racism, hopelessness, and physical functioning among Black American men and women: A cross-sectional test of two "weathering" hypotheses. Stigma and Health. https://doi.org/10.1037/sah0000568

Jones, K. (2022, January 10). How we can win: Race, history and changing the money game that's rigged: Paperback. Barnes

& Noble. https://www.barnesandnoble.com/w/how-we-can-win-kimberly-jones/1137541101

Metzger, I. W., Anderson, R. E., Are, F., & Ritchwood, T. (2021). Healing interpersonal and racial trauma: Integrating racial socialization into trauma-focused cognitive behavioural therapy for African American youth. Child Maltreatment, 26(1), 17–27. https://doi.org/10.1177/1077559520921457

Parsons, S., Collins, T. Z., & Cox, R. D. (2019). Race and Color in Louisiana: An Update on the Clark and Clark Doll Experiment. Journal of Race & Policy (Old Dominion University), 15(1), 24–53.

Racial differences in economic security: Housing. U.S. Department of the Treasury. (2022, December 6). https://home.treasury.gov/news/featured-stories/racial-differences-in-economic-security-housing

Reese, D. (2013). 5 Annie Turnbo Malone and African American Beauty Culture in the American West. In C. Warsh & D. Malleck (Ed.), Consuming Modernity: Gendered Behaviour and Consumerism before the Baby Boom (pp. 101-111). University of British Columbia Press. https://doi.org/10.59962/9780774824705-007

Richard, C. (2024). Jump Nyabinghi: Black Radical Militancy, Rastafarianism, and Jamaican Cultural Influence on Black America. Journal of Black Studies, 55(2), 117–138. https://doi.org/10.1177/00219347231213377

Seaton, E. K., Iida, M., & Morris, K. (2022). The Impact of Internalized Racism on Daily Depressive Symptoms Among

Black American Adolescents. Adversity and Resilience Science: Journal of Research and Practice, 3(3), 201–208. https://doi.org/10.1007/s42844-022-00061-1

Seider, S., Tamerat, J., Clark, S., & Soutter, M. (2017). Investigating Adolescents' Critical Consciousness Development through a Character Framework. Journal of Youth & Adolescence, 46(6), 1162–1178. https://doi.org/10.1007/s10964-017-0641-4

Skott, C., & Naum, M. (2019). Human Taxonomies: Carl Linnaeus, Swedish Travel in Asia and the Classification of Man. Itinerario, 43(2), 218–242. https://doi.org/10.1017/S016511531900024X

Smith, L. L. (2022). Speaking the Unspoken: Understanding Internalized Racial Oppression from the Perspective of Black Women Psychotherapists. Smith College Studies in Social Work (Taylor & Francis Ltd), 92(1), 48–72. https://doi.org/10.1080/00377317.2022.2026855

Tarlo, E. (2019). Racial hair: the persistence and resistance of a category. Journal of the Royal Anthropological Institute, 25(2), 324-348.

Willoughby, C. D. E. (2018). Running Away from Drapetomania: Samuel A. Cartwright, Medicine, and Race in the Antebellum South. The Journal of Southern History, 84(3), 579–614.

www.ingramcontent.com/pod-product-compliance
Lightning Source LLC
Chambersburg PA
CBHW050654270326
41927CB00012B/3021